Stop thinking like a freelancer
The Evolution of a $1m web designer

Copyright 2014. Published in the UK & Worldwide by Freelancelift Ltd.
All Rights reserved
ASIN: B00PJIDO9C

ISBN-13: 978-1503273146
ISBN-10: 1503273148

First edition

Liam Veitch, Author
Alec Ross & Morissa Schwartz, Editors
Tom Morkes, Insurgent Publishing.

About the author

Who cares, right? Well, if you insist.

A perennial business builder who 'finally got something to work', Liam Veitch has many strings to his bow, along with an equal amount of failures to recount. A web designer by trade and now founder at UK based web agency Tone (tone.co.uk) as well as freelancer community Freelancelift (freelancelift.com), this book comprises everything he wished he knew *first time around.*

In his own words, he did freelancing 'right this time' and this book comes from a realization that in the three years that have passed - this *second time around* as a freelancer - the business has generated over $1.1M. This debut, feature length book lays out the five phases of **evolutionary growth** that made this possible along with honest, action-oriented advice for implementing it in your own freelance business.

Oh, and he hates writing in third person.

Foreword

It's ironic that the final chapter added to a book is often the *'foreword'*. That is certainly the case here as I enter the final throws of this life-dominating project. It's been a blast. Completely exhausting but fun all the same; now I can't wait to show you what I came up with.

Between appearances on podcasts, launch planning, producing videos and the small matter of getting the written ideas - some 50,000 words - into a logical order I've also had the small matter of managing a business.

The purpose of this book is not to show you how to build *an agency*, nor is it to improve the actual service you're providing, I'm making the assumption this is already the best it can be. This book is here to help give a fresh perspective in a space dominated by mediocrity.

Most advice for freelancers sucks, you'll hear me say that a lot. Please don't mistake this for arrogance or elitism though, I am acutely aware all of this content is well-meaning, it's just for the most part it keeps us hemmed into a freelancer mindset.

I could have opted to entitle this book '101 ways to grow your freelance business' quite easily; maybe more people would have bought it.

Who knows, the point is, I didn't because I want more for you than that.

To do so would be to keep you thinking the same way you already are, bouncing around the freelancer echo chamber like a plucky, yet unlucky pinball. This book is for you if you want to be more than just "doing okay" this time next year.

Deep down we're all looking to achieve the same thing, freedom (in all its guises) and I've poured the last three months of my life into giving you the best chance of making that happen.

I've built something incredible from my tiny freelance business. I realized that chasing down ambiguous words like "growth" stopped me from putting in place constant, small goals.

I have a better word, *evolution* and I've witnessed all five phases of it. Mastering each will take you closer to your goals; all you have to do is stop thinking like a freelancer.

To the fire of ambition that lies within you

Learning the hard way: freelancing is rough

"F**k freelancing", I said.

It was 11 p.m. on a gloomy Saturday in February 2009, and the final 'no' in a series of four negative responses flashed into my inbox. This was prospective client work I'd pegged my hopes on winning. **I was officially done as a freelance designer.**

With no new work on the horizon and without a financial buffer, I'd reached the end. It was time to throw in the towel, call time out and drag my sorry ass in the direction of full-time employment.

The slippery slope was greased around 12 months earlier. Indeed, 2008 was a dark year for me; I had found myself peering over the edge financially on a number of occasions, playing the usual 'robbing Peter to pay Paul' games that everyone with an unstable income is familiar with.

I'd been self-employed for all of my adult life, doing what I supposed that *try-hard entrepreneurs* did, flipping from opportunity to opportunity without one ever *really* connecting.

I was finding it difficult to admit, or even articulate, that I had a weakness.

Something just wasn't right. No amount of "freelancer advice" (inverted commas intentional) seemed to make a difference.

The last few months of 2008 and the first few months 2009 would prove to be the final stretch of a pivotal downward spiral. I was a good designer, and my clients were generally happy with my work. I just couldn't get *enough clients* on a monthly basis to make freelancing pay.

In the end, I was consistently earning **less than I would as an employee** of someone else's business. As you probably know, *that* feeling and *that realization* really, truly sucks.

My freelance design venture was generally failing. Worse, it was dragging down my heart, soul and bank balance with it.

Shadowy figures

September 2008 was particularly somber, and it came to a head one murky Tuesday. I heard a rap on the door, which ordinarily I'd have ignored due to looming overdue bills. But I was expecting a package from a client, a delivery which I assumed would need a signature.

Wrong guess.

What stood before me was the archetypal grim reaper of finance. Head to toe in black, wearing a chunky bomber jacket and sporting a heavy build. Clipboard in hand and polished black steel-capped boots, which shone up from the damp doorstep.

A *bailiff* had arrived to take stock of my worldly possessions. Fortunately for me, I didn't have much to show at the time (if you can call that fortunate). Yet the humiliation of this ultimate invasion was something I'll never forget.

I managed to hold off the inevitable for a few more months, furiously spinning on hamster wheel until that final high pitch 'blip' of rejection hit my inbox in February.

And there I was. Staring at a blinking cursor, brooding over a way to reply without including an 'F' and a 'U'.

I had failed to stem the leak in my freelance business, and it was to prove fatal.

"F**k freelancing", I said.

Why you should read this book

This was a low point, sure. But, as I will explain in the following pages, I turned it around. That doesn't mean I'm on some self-indulgent ego-crusade to toot my own horn. After all, you don't care about me or my story. That's cool. I'm just another guy you found on the Internet.

But you *do* care about keeping the lights on and putting food on the table. You hate it when you can't be 100% sure that those responsibilities will be taken care of two months from now.

I understand that. That's why I wrote this book – and it's why you should read it.

I'm still *'in the field.'* I'm not some faceless, distant, self-proclaimed guru whose primary business is selling information to you instead of selling a service to clients.

I still head up Tone Agency. I still take on one freelance project per month, and I still hustle. Granted, I'm not a slave to money any more. But let's just say that I don't work four hours a week, either.

My intention is to describe my experiences and provide inspiration and practical advice for putting them to work in your business. These experiences have led to an enormous amount of financial freedom and professional predictability for me...

... *something I could only dream about before.*

A tie, a brave face and a turning point

Let's rewind back to 2009, when I figured my freelance career was toast.

I pulled down my website, and threw on a tie and a brave face. In March, I took up a position with a 400+ employee corporation on their digital team.

What I encountered was a *beast with a split personality*. What hid beneath the bureaucracy, rules and a herd of zombie employees was cutting-edge strategy, vision, big ideas and a ruthless pursuit of **growth.**

Since the 'dog-walking school' venture I started at 11 years old, I'd been involved in some sort of business almost continually. Yet I'd never really been *in* a business. There's a difference.

So while the fidgety, creative, freelancer side of me hated the stifling bureaucracy, the more instinctive entrepreneur within me was thriving.

I began to notice patterns, and slowly realized that this defining moment – the bailiff's fateful knock at the door – actually had a silver lining. ***This was how you 'did' business.*** I had acquired an insight to the inner workings of the corporate machine that I likely wouldn't have found while working by myself.

It was a resurgence of inspiration, and I devoured it raw. As the pieces of the jigsaw began to fall into place, the crescendo built.

I found myself at an all-staff meeting. It was in a long, cold conference room with 100 or so employees who had been summoned to listen to a lengthy presentation on the future of the business and its strategy.

While the zombies around me snored, doodled and generally did anything but listen, I was on the edge of my seat, a panting dog, tail wagging with ideas and brain whirring about how to translate all this information to a small-business context.

For me, this was solid gold. Half of me wanted to wave a hand in front of the eyes of my zombie colleagues to wake them up to the opportunities this insight could give them. The other, more selfish half of me wanted to absorb it all like a sponge, internalize it and put it into action immediately.

Then it hit me like a steam train. I had unearthed the weakness that led to my failure first time around. **I was**

thinking like a freelancer, and not thinking like a business. My narrow business horizon had prevented me from evolving and growing my way to success.

At the time, I wondered, what would happen if I took that same aggressive discipline toward a vision and market domination, and combined it with the agility, love and personality of a freelancer?

A vow to try again

I was 18 months into my corporate job and my restless mental cogs wouldn't stop spinning. I was connecting dots left and right, formulating a unique business outlook that would later become the *five phases* of this book.

With an embryonic version of the *freelancer evolutionary growth cycle* in hand, I set about putting together a new part-time design business. I was motivated by one vow: to **try again, and do it properly this time.**

This time I was a brand. This time, I was different. This time, I was building a business destined for success.

Despite the still-fresh trauma of previous failure, I set about building a venture that fused the world of cold, harsh, real-world business practice with the kind of creativity, passion and care only found in a small business.

From accounting to customer service, from marketing to production, I ran my part-time "just me" design business with the strategic precision of a publicly traded company.

I noticed an dramatic difference. My new approach was immediately validated.

- **Month 1** - I earned enough to cover my time to set up the business at a reasonable hourly rate;

- **Month 3** - I surpassed my monthly salaried income for the first time;

- **Month 5** - I closed a deal that earned me three times my monthly salaried earnings.

In that month, I earned $9,548. I scribbled that four-digit number all over my job wage slip, which totaled just over $3,000.

Something had to give.

A crossroads

I had a simple, yet critical choice. Red pill or blue pill. Easy or hard.

In one direction was a stable, above-average salary at a simple job with minimal stress, and semi-enjoyable work.

In the other direction was a completely unpredictable route I'd followed to failure once before. This path had a guarantee of uncertainty, an absence of security and the maximum amount of stress I could expose myself to.

"F**k it, back to freelancing", I said.

I'd been able to establish enough security with my one-person sideline business – at the time, offering web design for bands and the music industry – to take the measured leap.

On August 17, 2011, I founded Brandshank Ltd. as an official business entity.

I'm glad I did.

Just over three years ago I founded my "something" with nothing more than a laptop, a rented desk in a co-working space, ten digits at the end of two arms, and one vision. Today I have a self-sufficient, fun, growing web agency (Tone), along with other offshoots (Brandshank being one of them), all capable of operating – and growing – without my day-to-day presence.

I had to write this book. I had found the light that I'd lacked through all those dark years. I'd finally made freelancing work, and had $1,112,409.09 in revenues to show for it. **I'd successfully evolved.**

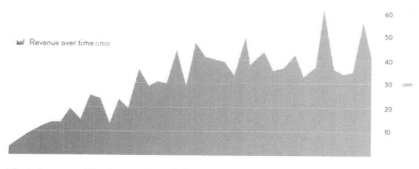

(Chart shows monthly sales over the period, to $1.1m in 3yr revenue)

Freelancing is tough enough already. So it's time for you to start thinking like a business. To **build a business that is evolution-ready** from the outset.

You may not want to build an agency like I did and this isn't the point of this book. You may not want to hire a team, and you may not want to deal with more than one client at a time. I accept that.

As we'll discover in this book, **growth is a relative concept.** It'll mean something different to you than it does to every other person picking up this book. One thing we can all agree on is that we need to feel momentum, a constant state of progression and at least a sense that we'll hit our goals one day. That's why I don't just call it "growth" any more, I call it *evolution* instead.

Growth vs Evolution

"For millions of years, mankind lived just like the animals. Then something happened which unleashed the power of our imagination."
Stephen Hawking

There are few words more ambiguous than "growth". I use the word carefully and only in precise context. Otherwise, it's a subjective can of worms.

Does "growth" mean growth in size? Growth in revenue? Growth in value? Growth in experience? Growth in success? Growth in reputation?

Or is it all of them? If so, which one do you tackle first? This cluster of grey areas often creates procrastination, especially with the one-person nature of a freelancer.

Sure, we want growth in revenue, but do we really want growth in size? We want to grow in experience, but some of us are happy being a boutique outfit. Do we really want *more* customers or just ones which pay more?

This often leads to an unhelpful tug-of-war between regurgitated points of view bounced around inside the tiny "freelancer blog" echo chamber. This just skews the issue and leads to a whole heap of nothing.

No growth in size, revenue, experience, value, success or reputation.

No action. No progression. Nothing, nothing, nothing.

Just blindly aiming for growth is no longer an option. We need to try something else. I have a new concept. I call it ***evolution.***

Evolution is worth aiming for. Evolution means constantly improving. Evolution is tangible, impactful, exciting. Growth is good, of course, but the word itself is easy to misinterpret and overanalyze. Evolution is worth pursuing.

You're too busy for bad news. If you're constantly improving through evolution, you build momentum and good news at every milestone.

When applied to business, evolution is the art of building something you can look back on in six months and say "Hey, that's different, that is an improvement."

Here's the big idea in 26 words:

This book will teach you how to stop thinking like a freelancer, start thinking like a business and evolve your way to your own, unique goals.

Your time to push forward

"I will go anywhere, provided it be forward."
David Livingstone, Explorer

At Freelancelift, I teach these principles and have been blown away by the response. I thrive on the effect these ideas have had on over 5,000 fellow freelancers who are all trying to push forward, innovate and evolve in a tough space.

The principles in this book are a combination of my story and the stories of other top-bracket freelancers who have broken away from the *up-then-down* income rollercoaster. I interviewed all of them in preparation for this book and on the Freelancelift podcast, so I could piece together the most comprehensive, honest guidance I could. All of whom are now firmly in the 'top bracket' I'd like to see you exist in. Some of them I now count as friends.

I have experienced all five phases of the *freelancer evolutionary growth cycle,* and in this book you'll read stories, examples and practical advice that will help you map out your own evolutionary path.

Your time is now. As a one-person business, it's easy to think that you're somehow exempt from that word... 'business'.

I'm here to tell you this is what keeps most freelancers thinking like, well, freelancers. Screw that! You have a product (your craft), you have outgoings, you have customers, you need to deliver your product efficiently, you need to find new clients and you need to turn a profit to survive.

Sound familiar? Yup, you're a business. It's the same for you as it is for Google, Facebook and MegaCorp Inc. So why do most freelancers limit themselves to run-of-the-mill freelancer blogs, same-same books and so-so advice that perpetuate the same message continually?

You need to think bigger. You need to stop thinking like a freelancer.

The freelancer evolutionary growth cycle

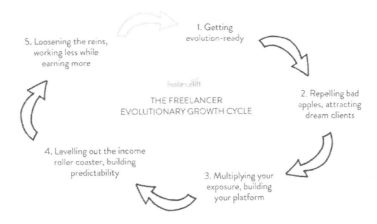

It starts by understanding that you should frame your growth as 'evolutionary', which can best be described as "always getting better". There are five distinct phases, but since "getting better" never stops, the process is cyclical.

What I'll teach you in this book will ensure that you can grow through these phases quicker and quicker with each revolution while making a real impact on your tiny business in the process.

You can expect to double or triple the revenue you're making with each lap of the cycle. Evolution never stops. Understanding this will make it easier for you to chart your progress and work on *what really matters* rather than endlessly debating about your interpretation of the word "growth".

You can cycle through these phases at your own pace. This doesn't have to be a year-long piece of work, so don't be too afraid to attack more than one evolutionary phase at once.

Just don't tell Charles Darwin you upended his theory.

What follows is a quick overview of each phase.

Phase I - Get evolution-ready

A typical comment I hear from freelancers is:

"I do okay, but feel like I'm treading water."

My answer generally goes like this: "I hear you, but think for a second. How do you *really* know how you're doing?"

Sure, your revenue is the same on average, and you feel there is a lack of progression there. But is your quality of life better? Do you have more freedom? Are you working less? Are you more skilled than you were last month? Is your pipeline looking healthier?

When looking at it with the right attitude, the issue really should not so much be a *lack of achievement*, but more *a lack of understanding* of the **stage of your development.**

An evolution-ready business owner has foundations for success, she understands what her vision is, she has mapped a strategy to get there, and she understands that "getting better" never stops.

In this phase, we'll address the underlying factors you need to have in place before even thinking about evolving your business. All this stuff – your mindset, your strategy, where you want to go – is often completely overlooked.

We're not talking about cumbersome, time-consuming business plans either. For a small, agile business, these are not worth the paper they're written on.

Things change quickly. We adapt to opportunities and make stuff up. Like that time you pretended you could do *that thing* for a client, just because you didn't want to say no and open the door for someone else – then frantically scoured Google to find a way to learn, quickly.

This is the best part: adapting, improving, learning, having fun plying our trade. It's the vibrancy that gets us out of bed in the morning. Yet, we still need to know the endgame – *"the why"*.

Why are we doing this? What are we aiming for? Why does that achievement matter? What does success look like?

If you don't know what you're aiming for, how will you ever know when you get there?

If your business isn't evolution-ready, you aren't taking the strategic steps required to *enforce* that upward trajectory.

When we fix that for you and you have clarity on what you can achieve, you can build a business around evolution, **not around you**. By doing so, you'll be empowered to be objective and understand just how far you've come.

Phase II - Repel bad apples, attract dream clients

I have an inconvenient truth to put to you. If you have lower-paying, frustrating, impatient, *throw-them-out-the-window* type clients, **it's your fault.**

In the large majority of cases, it's *you* who decides the caliber of client you get.

You attracted them with your positioning, *you* had the final say on the price, *you* drew out the deliverables, *you* agreed to the deadlines, and *you* control how you're perceived online.

I hate to break it to you. It's not them. It's you.

This phenomenon reminds me of the "quit hitting yourself" game we used to play with our siblings when we were kids. You're beating yourself around the head with your own brand, slapping all the fun out of freelancing.

This is compounded by the fact that you are spending an inordinate amount of time going out to find work, and only this current sorry crop of clients says yes.

Your freelance business has a fundamental issue with *perception*. You're attracting bad apples. It's time to change that.

A prospective client's perception of your pricing, value, quality, reliability and skill can *all be influenced*, and in most cases radically changed.

By engineering your professional image, you'll repel these bad apples and only attract the clients you want to work with. You'll build a pipeline of dream clients who *find you*, are relaxed and pay ten times more than the '*awkwards*'.

Phase III - Multiply exposure, build your platform

I know the feeling of hopelessly refreshing the screen of a virtually blank Google Analytics profile, only to see the blue-line chart keep looking more like low-lying hills than an epic mountain range.

About six months ago, I put together a free short book entitled "Why Nobody Knows your Name". Articulating the main issues in this way has helped make things a little clearer for everyone who downloaded it. But I wanted to go deeper.

Have you ever stopped to wonder how 'A list' freelancers ended up where they are? Was it a '*time in the game*' thing? Maybe. Was it luck? Maybe.

Or was it that they committed to *actually being vocal* in their space, building a reputation by providing value at every opportunity, and shouting about that value online?

A great online reputation can be a significant multiplier when it comes to setting a price for your work, so it pays to get it right.

Phase IV - Level out the income rollercoaster, build predictability into the model

Some weeks are great, but in others you feel the pinch. The difficulty is that you want the *good* weeks to be more frequent, but instead it's more bad weeks than good. This up-and-down uncertainty is usually the reason freelancers give for throwing in the towel.

So why do we allow this? Why do we work so hard to win a client, then happily bid them goodbye after the project is over?

Then why don't we diversify our channels of income?

The difficulty is that freelancing (when done the way we're *told to*) is an inherently unpredictable game. We drag this disadvantage around with us like an invisible ball and chain, yet we change nothing.

You should be building relationship opportunities with clients and nurturing long-term partnerships to increase the likelihood that they will spend their dollars to hire you again and again. You should create side projects that deliver revenue even in slow weeks. You should understand the importance of customer lifetime value.

Money isn't everything, but it brings security, comfort, reassurance and the material things in life.

If the financials of your business are stable, you can enjoy your craft and do something you love, while knowing that the financial elephant in the room is at least well fed.

Phase V – Loosen the reins, work less, earn more

Freelancers wear lots of hats. We occupy every role in our businesses. It's exhausting. We're responsible for sales, marketing customer service, production, accounts and everything in between.

We certainly didn't apply for this 'Chief Octopus' role. When it gets in the way of focusing on what really matters, it becomes a real threat to the business.

Have you ever wondered why you wear all these hats? Are you the best person for *that* job? Does it contribute to your bottom line? Could you move that along to someone less qualified, but who has more time to dedicate to it?

Your business has an infrastructure problem. It simply isn't equipped to deal with life *without you in it*. What processes are in play, and how could these be made more efficient? Could you do things more quickly, hire a remote team, or take advantage of specialized software?

In this phase, we'll seek to build a well-oiled machine that enables you to offload about 30% of your day-to-day time commitments, without losing revenue.

The best part about evolution is that even reaching the end of the final phase doesn't signal the end for you. You'll be earning more, yes, but you need to re-map your goals and get yourself evolution-ready all over again.

I'm excited to walk you through this. So let's begin.

Download full versions of the tools, resources and worksheets which support this book, by heading to freelancelift.com/book

Phase I

Get evolution-ready

What is your intent?

As the hills rolled by, Jeff and his wife were reaching the end of their cross Country jaunt from New York to Seattle. With tired eyes they reached their destination, turning the ageing blue sedan into the driveway of their new home.

What stood before Jeff was the start of a new chapter in his life, it was 1994 and he'd just quit his *'fairly well paid'* job in New York to work on something more meaningful.

Jeff was born in Albuquerque New Mexico, USA and had a relatively normal upbringing. He had a keen interest in computing that would eventually take him to Princeton University.

Sure, Jeff was smart but his peers were too. Jeff though had something his classmates did not, **a vision, backed by intent.**

Intent is drive; intent is passion and a yearning towards an audacious goal. Intent is what inspires us to keep going even on the bad days and its something I want to instill in you.

As Jeff lifted open the garage door with a creak, he glanced down at the paper he'd scribbled on through the duration of the trip. Staring back was his intent, his vision to create *'Earth's biggest bookstore'* from that few square feet of cold garage. He'd given up everything.

Sure, he wasn't completely certain how he would make that rise - especially with the uncertainty of the new world of *'The Internet'*. Of course there were bumps along the way and there would be challenges to come, but **that vision and fire** didn't change.

You see Jeff built a business that was *evolution-ready* from the outset with an unflinching vision of where he wanted it to go.

That mission still stands today, and from his garage he created something remarkable. Jeff Bezos is the (now billionaire) founder, CEO and Chairman of Amazon.com.

In this phase the objective is to figure out **what we want to achieve** and what will need to change to make that so.

Your 'one-page of intent'

The stories, advice and ideas which follow will give you the searching questions required to achieve the insight, clarity and perspective you'll need to complete **a simple strategy sheet**, your 'one page of intent'.

This purposeful plan we'll complete at the end of the chapter so for now just absorb the concepts as they arise and we'll recap and make it actionable at the end.

Being *reactive* in our business exploits will only take us so far. It's time *get deliberate, commit to getting better* and leverage the power of **evolutionary intent.**

Preparing for a constant state of improvement

I established in the previous chapter that "growth" is an extremely subjective concept. I get an equivalent 'shudder' when it comes to defining other such meaningless concepts. *"Moving to the next level"* they say, *"Taking it a step further"* they cry, *"Scale up"*, they chant.

Like a raucous stock market floor, these words are all noise and no meaning unless you provide appropriate context or attach them to *something meaningful* in your life and in your business. When these statements are not quantified it leaves us grasping for the next big move, in a position I call 'maintenance mode'.

If you can't immediately point to a specific action you took this week that furthered and evolved your business then you'll probably find you're in maintenance mode with your freelance business. Stuck on a plateau. Static, yet furiously spinning the hamster wheel, unclear of the most effective 'to do' action.

I want to help you break from that habit of churning out the same actions day to day, Maintenance Mode is the root cause of that frustrating 'treading water' feeling.

The goal of this book is to get you thinking in terms of evolution, of living in a constant state of improvement, of **continually getting better,** overcoming maintenance mode and achieving positive action.

It's up to you to determine what 'getting better' actually means to you though:

- Does 'getting better' mean more money? Great, how much?
- Does 'getting better' mean more clients? How many?
- Does 'getting better' mean working less? Perfect, what will you do with the time?
- Does 'getting better' mean working on projects you really enjoy? What work makes you most happy, and with what type of client?

As you can see when you talk about 'getting better' or evolving as a freelance business, you will get one answer from one person, and a different answer from another.

You need to prepare yourself for charting what that means to **you**.

There is no *one size fits all* guidance here. We're all looking for that piece of the jigsaw that'll fall in our lap, more often than not it doesn't happen, so take advice and run with it, try stuff.

It's a common trait of the ultra-successful to focus on *continually getting better* rather than *being the best*. In 1994 Barnes & Noble were the undisputed heavyweight champions of the book world, did that stop Jeff Bezos?

This is why I advocate *continual testing, regular evaluation and structured improvement* as an approach. This needn't be scary though, I appreciate that terminology smacks of the 'buzzwords' we're trying to move away from.

What we're talking about here is a **continual growth towards a goal** (whatever that goal is for your specific situation) and regular review of some key benchmarks to ensure you're getting a regular pat on the back. Understand that its *up to you alone* to ensure you're continually improving and you should know where you'd like that improvement to lead.

No journey succeeds without a map

I love to travel. In the past 18 months alone I've visited four continents and clocked up 48,427 miles - that's equivalent to flying the circumference of the planet, twice.

Throughout all of these trips there has been one constant (and I'm not talking about the extreme discomfort and poor quality food); each journey had a **defined endpoint**, a destination to mark the trip complete.

Had I not marked out a destination, and commenced the journey without a map or a clear path to my endpoint I would have been a mere nomad.

The Nomadic lifestyle won't help your business

In business, a nomadic lifestyle - continually being *reactive* to environments, moving on when times get tough to an *indeterminate location* – almost always ends in failure.

Whether this is a slow downward spiral (in my case 2 years in the making) or a chain of events more swift and severe the fact remains. If you do not have a map (a vision, with strategy outlined) or a destination (a clear business goal or objective) you will find it difficult to succeed in business.

Remember, you are not exempt from 'being in business' just because you're a freelancer. This mentality keeps freelancers from breaking free of *the up-then-down* income roller coaster cycle, boxes us into maintenance mode and produces that feeling of 'treading water' and ultimate dissatisfaction with our craft.

With these higher-level concepts addressed, lets move into some specific examples and actionable ideas.

Know where you want to go (ditch the business plan)

It's fortunate that the 'business plan' as it was (an overly complex, cumbersome, often pointless exercise) is a thing of the past. Who wants to put together vague forecasts and meandering analyses over 50 pages anyway?

At Tone and my other brick & mortar businesses every time I've been forced to complete one (banking, funding) they have been out of date and superseded almost as quickly as they're created.

In his book 'Rework' Jason Fried - founder of Basecamp/37Signals - advocates a 'lean approach' to business objectives. Working to small, short term goals and knocking them down regularly to achieve a constant state of momentum.

In this phase, we'll work towards creating our '***one page of intent***'. A simple, short and adaptable version of the *tired ol'* business plan.

Armed with this briefest of maps you can make *short term goals* that ensure you can continually reflect on "getting better"

Your objective, what does evolution mean to you?

Before embarking on any business venture that key question is crucial. Indeed, so crucial and so seemingly obvious it's often glossed over as a no brainer. A normal conversation with the freelancers I speak to when I'm coaching and supporting would go something like this:

"Well, evolution to me means more money of course?"
Really? Is that the main reason, why is that important?

"Umm so I can live well and buy nice things"
Okay, I guess we're getting closer, but why is that important?

"Well, so I can spend more time with my family, work less, go on vacations and drive a great car"

Now we're talking – money is the means to the end you're dreaming of. So how much money do you need on a monthly basis to make that happen?

"I'd say to cover my costs, plus living expenses, a car lease plus an amount disposable for holidays and such I'd need about $8,000 per month."

So "earning $8,000 per month to live well and do things with family" is the goal (in this example) not 'earning more money'.

This should be what you look to as 'evolution'.

Both statements technically say the same thing, yet one will **inspire action** while the other is too vague and impossible to measure your progress against.

You should see your business as the vehicle for making that journey from where you are now to living the life you want to. That is to say, like any journey **you can only really begin once you've established exactly where you're going.**

Try it for yourself, ask why you set out freelancing in the first place, what does evolution mean to you? Then ask "and why is that important?" 4 or 5 times to arrive at your real, underlying, specific goal.

It's the same whether your underlying goal is to have more time, more money, more satisfaction in your craft. You can always dig deeper to **quantify the specifics.**

We'll make this your *destination*, to be utilized within your one page of intent.

Download full versions of the tools, resources and worksheets which support this book, by heading to freelancelift.com/book

What is stopping you achieving your vision already?

It was a Wednesday I recall, the rain tapped on the window and it was just 'another day' at my corporate job. I was called into a meeting to strategize on how the digital team could help the business be more visible to its customers.

We were immediately introduced to a business management concept popularized by author Eliyahu M. Goldratt, the **Theory of Constraints (TOC).**

This was new information to me, so I made it a mission to digest and understand it and I mark this experience as another lightbulb moment in my evolution to where I am today.

The summary concept of TOC is that *a lack of achievement towards a business objective almost always has one converging root cause.* There is a whole lot more to it than this, but when working online we can pull it back to some simple data to understand how to reverse this root constraint into a specific objective.

Example

If your earnings goal is $8,000 per month and you currently make $4,000 you have a need to **double your revenue**, so what is preventing you?

If you are missing your revenue targets because your customers aren't paying enough what is that a symptom of? Poor positioning? Lack of exposure?

So why do you have a lack of exposure? What could you be doing differently in your space to remedy that? Is it the fact that you don't have an effective web or social presence?

It starts with benchmarking

You'll find it difficult to pluck this out of the air, so to assist I've mapped out the four core data points you should be taking notice of, you should look to benchmark how you fare (take data from the previous few months) in order that we clearly know our starting point.

1. Getting attention

If nobody reaches your site, or even knows your name you may be facing obstacles getting attention, what specifically is stopping you getting the attention you need?

Example response: I currently attract 500 visits per month to my site / portfolio

2. Converting attention to leads

Whether you're working online or offline, the need to build leads is insatiable. How can you get the volume of leads (enquiries / briefs / inbound calls) you need to support the growth you need?

Example response: I currently convert 2% of these visits into leads (10 leads)

3. Converting leads to customers

Whether this is improving your sales process, strengthening your lead nurturing or upping your conversion rate you will have obstacles in this area if you aren't hitting the numbers.

Example response: Of every five leads I win one new client – I have a 20% lead to customer rate (2 customers)

4. Managing a steadily increasing average order value

Put simply, you have the ability to re-engineer the way you look at pricing (which we look at in Phase II) so you should map out what your benchmark number is, in order that we can make an impact on it.

Example response: My average project fee is about $2,000

Could you improve each by just 20%?

Here is the interesting thing; to increase your earnings by 100% you only need to **improve in each of the four areas by 20%.**

Here are some other combinations, which will deliver you that same end result, to double your income. Which one seems most realistic to your skillset?

- ✓ Increase average project fee by 100%
- ✓ Increase traffic and visit-to-lead conversion rate by 30% each
- ✓ Increase traffic by 100%
- ✓ Increase traffic and average project fee by 30% each
- ✓ Improve all four areas by 20%

There are some areas you'll immediately be more comfortable in, for example you may be confident of using some of the ideas in this book to double your project rate (hint: Phase II) or you may have expertise driving traffic yourself or want to leverage the ideas in Phase III of this book (multiplying exposure).

Your particular objective(s) will ultimately depend on the destination you choose.

These **specific objectives** should be added to your one-page of intent. They're deliberately driven by data, so you can measure yourself against them on an ongoing basis.

Be the specialist (even when you're not)

It's a common truism that the smaller your potential pool of customers the higher your likelihood of making the sale. This feels somewhat counter-intuitive and something it took me a while to figure out. Bigger pool of clients = more chance of making a customer right? *Wrong.*

Especially in the freelancing game when you focus on 'everyone' you're just opening yourself out to competition from all over the world.

You can be sure that if your potential market size is only handful of businesses or individuals there will be a lot less competition.

You should make it clear who you really serve, who will buy your service and what are their sensitivities? What are their desires, beliefs, fears and how does your service slot in? This is something we dive deep on in Phase II however to be evolution-ready you need to be prepared for it, up front.

In 2004 **Joanna Wiebe** of Copyhackers headed into the big wide world of freelance content writing. At first, she referred to herself as a *'creative writer'* and points this out as one of the mistakes that set her progress back somewhat.

Over the years, Joanna has refined this message, into the super-specific:

'Conversion copywriter for businesses in the startup and marketer space who want to boost sales and revenue from web pages'

In doing so, Joanna has reduced her potential pool of clients from millions of businesses that may want 'creative writing support' down to probably a few hundred who want this *specific type* of copy.

Joanna now regularly charges upwards of $400 per hour for her copy critique service.

A lot of marketing and customer acquisition centers on *perception*. Is your prospective client more likely to go for the freelancer that has demonstrable experience and a roster of successes with businesses like theirs? Or with the freelancer who has experience across all sectors, often with work in completely different markets to theirs?

In big business these are known as 'verticals'. Specific market sectors in which a supplier can **be a specialist, for a more bespoke overall service**. As a specialist in a particular field, you can command a much higher project fee for your service.

If your experience to date is quite varied, there are still ways of applying this same methodology.

If you have clients in different sectors that you can loosely group together why not create landing pages or sub sections of your site, which address the concerns, needs and pains this specific vertical has?

Grouping your past experience in this way ensures you can still be the specialist, even when you're not.

It's even possible to build out your experience in a particular sector into a sub-brand (utilizing the same 'one page of intent' principles) in order that you can maximize your effectiveness and the likelihood of attracting a higher quality of client. This is something I did with Brandshank.

My first time around as a freelancer I was 'just a web designer'. Like a low-rate waiter, I served anybody with money.

It was only when I created a brand around '*web design for the music industry*' that it began to fall into place. I had better clients, I could bill more per client and the jobs were more efficient to produce as the features and objectives were similar.

Add to this the pure satisfaction of working in a sector you *actually enjoy* and it's a recipe for a profitable, fulfilling business life.

So even if you have a main brand right now you should consider grouping your experience into a sub-brand so that you can fine tune your prospective audience and have a much stronger chance of a sale.

In your one-page of intent, map out how your service could be **specialized into a certain sub-sector**, in phase II we'll look to actually reposition your message to this audience.

The difference between you and everyone else is?

It was a bumpy flight I recall as the journey shuddered into its second hour. I was midway through my first exposure to the wonders of 450mph travel with a spot just behind the wing, the window seat I had so coveted.

It was absolutely fascinating and I stared with amazement, a nine-year-old vision of concentration. Cloud by cloud, watching hills & mountains floating by beneath, the ground so far away yet so clear and crisp on this summer day.

This was something *truly different*, the awe inspired from that first trip I will never forget.

Just 20 years later I hop aboard the same flight, barely even considering whether I was going to occupy a window seat.

As the plane takes off; a sudden "clunk". The oddly shaped plastic of the window is shuttered down and I barely bat an eyelid.

The same ground floats beneath, the same wonderment of drifting through cloud lies outside and in that sense, nothing has changed. Yet I don't care that I'm staring at faded grey plastic instead.

What was once an awe inspiring, *truly different* experience is now commonplace, almost tedious and a 'necessary' addition to every trip.

Your prospective clients are jaded and tired too of their experience. The process of finding a freelancer (a once awe inspiring experience, like the first email you ever received, communicating and connecting with specialists from across the globe) is now commonplace.

To go back to the analogy, common "flight" just doesn't cut it any more; you need to inspire a perception of difference around your service. You need to *go Galactic.*

It starts by understanding that in 2015 - and beyond - **clients don't care about you.**

As in, *they don't care at all.*

Clients don't care, at least not yet

Now that the web is so central to our lives, it becomes more and more difficult to stand out. Prospective clients – like most of us – have become much more selfish in their consumption of information.

Understanding that clients don't care about you, your story or your qualifications will be the key to putting together a message that resonates with the specific audience we've already identified.

In a recent chat I had with Brennan Dunn, we talked specifically about this issue. Indeed, Brennan managed a larger consultancy before deciding to go freelance and now tells his story via his podcast and books. Here's what he says on the issue:

"Nobody was ever hiring me just because I knew how to write code, they're hiring us to solve a problem that exists in their business. The coding was the medium to get to that goal, when I focused on the goal rather than the skill it made it easier to justify my services as an investment."

– Brennan Dunn on Freelancelift Q&A

It is you who decides whether you remain part of the freelance masses. By looking like the herd, sounding like the herd, congregating with the herd you have no choice but to be considered as *the herd*.

Only you can change this. As freelancers join the herd, some break away but the main body of cattle remains the same. You should put together a set of values, differentiating factors and a message that demands you be considered differently.

Sure, you're a writer... but does a client care that you type at 10,000 words per minute? What about that random Tokyo skyline you have as your main slider image? You're a designer, clients want to see that but do they care enough to look at superfluous bar charts marking your effectiveness with CSS and jQuery? Nope.

So what do you provide - in a language they can compute – compared to the other options they've seen?

In all-too-many cases freelancers wax lyrical about the features of their service (I write really well, I design really well). When you take a step back and look at this objectively, why should they care?

You should address it in the context of your client; address the features and benefits *as they relate to them* and their business success.

A simple Google search give you an example of how jaded your prospective client is:

- If you're a designer, 891,000 of your competitors also "specialize in building websites"
- As a writer 635,000 of your peers also consider themselves a "content writing expert"

Language like this is so overused it becomes invisible to the client and just blends in to the background. Generic, disconnected words like this serve only the freelancer, in phase II we'll rework your messaging so that it serves your prospective client, too.

Speaking to a worldview, not a demographic

It's up to you to figure out what the primary purpose and primary benefit of your service is, through the client's eyes.

Clients don't care about you, or your story yet, they will do once they know you and have worked with you, until then they **only care how you can help them solve a business problem they are having.**

It's the difference between (real-life example):

"We make websites"

vs.

"We boost your revenue by designing websites that convert"

Which one is more likely to inspire action on the part of the prospect?

With that said, what do you do differently? Why should you be considered new, when set against the backdrop of the thousands of other freelancers as a prospect could choose?

You have a great opportunity to start down a path 90% of freelancers will not tread, to tune in to the worldview frequency of your prospective client and make the likelihood of sale much greater.

- What do they think they need?
- What else are they trying?
- What is their general perception of businesses like yours?

You should add your response to the one-page of intent (download an editable Word/Google Docs version here).

The purpose of laying out such a brief plan of attack is to actually leave room for change, for deviating away from your original plan as you learn more about prospects and dig deeper into all of these areas throughout the book.

In Phase II we'll look to put *this difference* into practice, flow it into every touchpoint a client will experience prior to working with you.

Taking yourself on as a client

I've said it before and I'll say it again, most advice for freelancers sucks. You'll often find same-same advice gobbling your time, perpetuated by voices whose primary business is selling you information, rather than services to clients.

With Freelancelift I began by reaching out to podcast guests a little differently. They had to meet the criteria I was looking for, namely that they had *been there done that* as a service provider, yet had widened their own net outside of that freelancer advice echo chamber.

Throughout all of these discussions there is a common trait, a **'get shit done'** mentality. If you're going to make this work for you and your business, if you genuinely are evolution-ready then you have to take the development of yourself and your business outlook seriously.

Imagine for a second, a new client lands in your lap, wanting to hire you for 4-5 hours every week. You'd leap headfirst into the opportunity. You'd easily have capacity to fit that in, regardless of how busy things got because *you had to,* there was money and client satisfaction relying on it.

Over the course of 6 months this gig would land you $5,000, maybe even $10,000 in revenue. You would bust a gut to make **every cent valuable to the client** and you can be darn sure you'd improve the business of the client and provide great opportunities for them and their business, far outweighing their investment.

Why then, are we so reluctant to invest that 4-5 hours a week in furthering the most important business of all, *our own*? Putting in place infrastructure changes that have the potential to deliver not just $5-10k over a 6-month period, but $5-10k *a month* for several years to come.

I refer to this as *taking yourself on as a client*; a bossy, firm-but-fair client who won't let you get off with skipping the odd hour. In a recent Q&A call Corbett Barr, founder at Fizzle.co had this to say:

"As a freelancer, you should be able to say: For x hours per week I'm going to be working on my 'Me Project', creating content and building things that are going to be better for my business in the long term."

- Corbett Barr on Freelancelift Q&A

By working this way you can allow, then justify time spent on developing and building the most important brand you'll ever work for... yourself.

Justin Jackson, founder at ProductPeople and epic writer at JustinJackson.ca coined the phrase **JFDI** (just f**ing do it) and in that vein talked at length on a recent podcast about his **"week of hustle"** concept.

"I found it funny [on spending time away and at conferences] that we had space to do that and be uncontactable for a few days or a week, yet we couldn't find a way to take that same time out and work on our own projects."

"What if I just set aside time, put on my out of office and worked on something small enough that I could finish it in one week or a few days"

- Justin Jackson on Freelancelift Q&A

How can you embrace the idea of 'taking yourself on as a client' in your own business? Can you designate a set day, a few hours or a period of time to work on your 'Me Project'?

It is essential to define and ring-fence this time. Whether its Sunday evenings, Monday 7am or Wednesday afternoon figure out when you can block it in.

Amy Hoy is a coder, speaker, product builder and all-round star of the freelance space and had this spark of inspiration to give:

"The best advice I can give is to free up one day a week, its epic... whether its all at once or two hours per day just do it, you can make total changes in your business that way."

- Amy Hoy on Freelancelift Q&A

So, what time will you put aside to *JFDI*?

Be accountable for achieving goals, regularly

By reading this book (and following through by completing as many actions as you can) you're making a commitment to *evolving your business*. To help you make this mindset shift, you should understand the science of small wins.

Teresa Amabile is a Professor of Business Administration at Harvard Business School. In 2011, following years of research and on-the-ground experiments she released her watershed book, *The Progress Principle*.

In it, she outlined that **incremental progress against defined goals** was a key psychological trigger for maximizing motivation.

You don't need to be a Harvard Professor to relate to the positive mental impact momentum like this has. That new keyboard shortcut you just picked up, the piece of work you just completed in record time, the realization that you cooked that meal better than you did last time.

Every one of these 'mini fist pumps' builds happiness and motivation as each is directly related to achievement. We're programmed to take hope and happiness from every achievement almost equally, regardless of the size.

Doesn't it make sense therefore to make sure the wins come regularly?

If you are setting yourself huge, unwieldy goals that stretch months and years into the future you're constantly pulling yourself wearily *towards* something, rather than bouncing *away from* a previous win.

If you break down larger goals into more manageable sub-objectives and give yourself a constant (ideally weekly) pat on the back for a job well done you have the momentum required to give you sustained motivation, even when times are tough.

So how often will you measure your progress?

Committing to evolution

Do you ever wonder why once-powerful businesses that monopolized a generation now only occupy a fraction of their market?

- In 2015 would you choose a Hoover over a Dyson?
- Why has Internet Explorer's market share been obliterated?
- Why is Nokia faced with bankruptcy while Apple is the most 'valuable business in history'?

Think about that for a second. *The most valuable business in history.* No business before or after it has done more for innovation in technological products.

Where was Microsoft while all this was happening? In big business, just as in freelancing if you're not moving forward your competition will **ensure** you're moving backward.

All of the brands I mentioned above were market leaders at their height globally, but they failed to commit to evolution, languished, then as a direct consequence fell behind to competition. In these extreme cases, the sleepy giants were still lacing their running spikes while their competition stood atop the podium collecting Gold with a clenched fist.

It comes back to that feeling of treading water, of holding your business back in *'Maintenance Mode'* due to a lack of positive action. I want to help you commit to being **evolution-ready**. If you've digested the ideas set out in this chapter you'll be in a position to complete your one page of intent, this will provide a set of guiding lights as you launch into the next phase of your growth.

But first, some bad news

Hopefully by now you're charged up and ready to do this, but I have an obligation to give you the bad news:

Most that start this book won't end up following it through. They will not evolve their business into something that transcends their current position.

If you take action on the information you have within this book, you have the best possible chance at growing something incredible from your tiny business. The alternative is to slip back into maintenance mode and the instability of the income roller coaster.

It will take some thought and focus to get this right, some three to five hours per week of 'taking yourself on as a client' and committing to evolution, but the upside renders this time investment insignificant.

If you're still with me, let's do this. What follows are the questions outlined in your one page of intent. (download an editable Word/Google Docs version here)

Finalizing your one page of intent

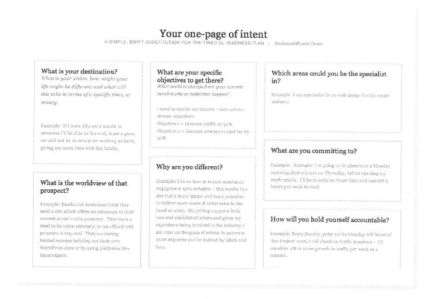

1. What is your destination?

What is your vision, how might your life might be different and what will this take in terms of a specific time, or money.

Example: If I have $8,000 a month in revenues I'll be able to live well, lease a great car and not be so reliant on working so hard, giving me more time with the family

2. What are your specific objectives to get there?

What needs to change from your current benchmarks to make that happen?

Example: I need to double my income – here are my chosen objectives:
*   Objective 1 = Increase traffic by 30%*
*   Objective 2 = Increase average project fee by 30%*

3. Which areas could you be a specialist in?

If you have areas you're currently serving which can be grouped, add them here. Or if there is an area you're particularly comfortable in you can include that too.

Don't be afraid to take more than one at this stage.

Example: I can specialize in on web design for the music industry

4. What is the worldview of that prospect?
Combine answers from questions like the ones below, to draw out a picture of the worldview of this prospect.

- What do they think they need?
- What else are they trying?
- What is their general perception of businesses like yours?

Example: Bands and musicians think they need a site which offers an extension to their current social media presence. They have a need to be taken seriously, so an official web presence is required. They are having limited success building out their own WordPress sites or by using platforms like Squarespace. They perceive web designers to either provide generic designs or be overly expensive vs DIY options.

5. Why are you different?
Taking a lead from your answers in number 4, how can you reverse some of these worldview aspects and position yourself as *different to the 99%?*

Example: I know how to ensure maximum engagement with websites – this results in a site that's more 'sticky' and has a potential to deliver more music & ticket sales to the band or artist. My pricing supports both new and established artists and given my experience being involved in the industry I am clear on the goals of artists, to generate more exposure and be noticed by labels and fans.

6. What are you committing to?

Put simply, what are you putting into this? Are you going to invest in your 'Me Project'? If so, what is the maximum you can commit to per week and when will that be? Even if its an hour a week, make it really specific.

Example: I'm going to do 3hours on a Monday morning then 2 hours on Thursday, before opening my work emails. I'll be in early on those days and commit 5 hours per week in total

7. How are you going to hold yourself accountable?

How often will you look back on results and what specifically will you monitor?

Example: Every Sunday, prior to the Monday AM burst of 'Me Project' work I will check on traffic numbers – I'll consider 2% or more growth in traffic per week as a success. Then I'll give myself a beer for every project I win over 50% of my benchmark. I'm looking to hit my destination within 6 months.

Once you have this brief map of intent created, it's time to move on to the next phase.

Download full versions of the tools, resources and worksheets which support this book, by heading to freelancelift.com/book

Phase II

Repel bad apples, attract dream clients

"People inspire you or they drain you.
Pick them wisely."
Hans F Hansen

After the third call of the day, I think he could sense my patience was waning. As a designer, there are only so many times you can be asked to increase the size of a logo. With unflinching diplomacy, I suggested it might be more efficient to describe his desired changes in an email, rather than take them one by one over telephone.

The client - let's call him Mr. B. Apple - duly agreed. I carefully hung up, thankful that I'd been able to convince him to use a less disruptive communication channel.

An hour or so passed before I spotted a red blink from the corner of my mobile phone signifying an SMS (this was when people actually owned BlackBerry technology). The text read, *"I've sent the email, could you let me know when you've been able to check it?"*

"Sure, I'll get on it," I replied, finally feeling I'd cracked the bad apple communication code.

I raised a lukewarm tea toward my lips and slurped a mouthful while my mail loaded. I almost spat it out as thirteen fateful words blinked back:

"Email as requested, please call me when you have a minute to take next feedback."

I could have cried.

We've all had them, bad-apple clients. Your heart sinks each time your inbox pings with yet another dreaded (and unnecessary) reminder for an update. It drags down your morale and starts to make you wonder why you took the project in the first place.

But you're in too deep to turn back, and there's no sign of light at the end of the tunnel. How did this happen?

Unfortunately this scenario probably sounds familiar. The harsh fact, though, is that bad-apple clients **are grown, not inherited.**

It doesn't *just happen.* Lower-quality clients aren't dropped at your door by a White Stork. You attract them. Your messaging, brand touchpoints, environment and your previous experience bring them to you.

So the responsibility for growing these clients lies squarely with you, for better or worse. In this section, I want to make sure it's the former.

Have you ever considered the early warning signals of good and bad clients?

Think about the clients who were a joy to work with, and the ones who were a pain. What are the characteristics of each? Where did their enquiry originate? What were their main concerns in the pre-sales phase? What questions did they ask that others did not?

The good news is that client quality can be engineered. Moreover, the work you do to repel bad apples will make you irresistible to dream clients.

You'll never change who *they* are and what they stand for, but you can change who *you* are when it comes to the factors that prospective clients consider when looking to work with you.

It starts with understanding the power of perception.

Perception of value

Just six years ago, BMW wrestled the Rolls Royce brand away from Volkswagen. The takeover was hostile, a dogfight until the last. Neither side stood to gain much in terms of raw profit from existing vehicle sales, but the battle remained.

Once Rolls Royce was under BMW control, the motivation for the takeover became clear. That same year, the *Rolls Royce Ghost* made its debut on the global stage. This was the first Rolls vehicle released under BMW's ownership, and it was developed in record time.

Almost too quickly, it would seem. At the same time, there was a more muted release from the German manufacturers. This one announced the new BMW 7 series. In fact, these two vehicles, very different in aspiration and perceived brand value, had a common denominator.

The **engine was the same,** as was one in every four parts.

The Rolls commanded a $300,000 price tag, while the BMW vehicle sold for just $100,000. Was one vehicle – with the same power, same engine built by the same manufacturer and similar parts – really worth *three times* the other?

Of course not. Yet the Rolls Royce had the *perception of value* on its side. The messaging, positioning and the aspirational nature of the Rolls combined with the goodwill and heritage associated with the legendary brand allowed the manufacturer to bill the end user 200% more.

You should understand that this 'brand engineering' is not the exclusive reserve of big business. On occasions, we bill *100 times more* at Tone than I did in my early days as a freelancer.

Is the product itself 100x better? No. Is the positioning and framing 100x better? Yes. Is the audience 100x better? Absolutely.

The iPhone 5S was manufactured at a production cost of $213 per handset by Apple. The Nokia Lumia 900 cost $209 to build, roughly the same. The Nokia carried a more effective camera and was considered by many to offer superior technology.

But the iPhone carried an impression of value, purveyed by an irresistible brand with huge amounts of intrinsic value and a framing of excellence on its side. So its $699 retail price tag was no surprise.

With the Lumia, Nokia struggled to justify a price tag of $369. This perception and value factor allowed Apple to justifiably bill almost twice as much as its competitor.

This perception can be engineered. Ultimately, it's up to you to define your value. You set your price, and accept the terms that come with it. You might feel you don't have a choice in it, that your rate is set by a fair market value.

I'm here to tell you that impression is incorrect.

Like the Rolls Royce, BMW and Apple examples, it's in your power to increase your rate by over 100% (or more) by understanding the importance of value perception.

How perception plays into pricing

Whether you buy into it or not, pricing is almost always value-led. The price you are comfortable paying for something is directly related to the value you *feel* you'll get from it. If everyone bought on price alone, without appreciation of value, we'd all drive a Datsun.

Therefore, if your price is deemed too high, in your clients' eyes your value is deemed too low for your pricepoint. The amazing paradox here is that **you control the value your client perceives**. Consequently, it is *you* who dictates whether a price is too high.

If you commit to building an optimal brand perception, you'll be in a considerably stronger position as a business.

During this phase we'll address the three main influences on building a perception that repels bad apples and attracts dream clients. These are your messaging, your brand touchpoints, and your relevant experience.

Your messaging

Earlier in the book I introduced the idea of *differentiation*, setting yourself apart from the thousands of other freelancers that a client could select. I'm sad to say that in my experience, this one area is completely overlooked by 90% of freelancers.

You have an opportunity to tell a story about the impact you can make to the lives of your dream client. Don't squander it. It's more than just a headline or website copy – it's a concerted effort across every inch of your brand to build a frame around you and your service and to ensure every paragraph makes the likelihood of a sale greater.

Brand touchpoints

A brand is not 'a logo', nor is it even strictly 'design'. A brand is an experience, a feeling, a sense and a vibration that oozes out of every interaction (however fleeting) between your business and a prospective client. *Tangible* mechanisms like a logo, a name, design, website content, proposal documents and others, are the vehicles that create that *intangible* experience.

It's vital that every touchpoint works in your favor. Each one must tell your story, attract the interest of dream clients, and communicate efficiently with current clients.

Relevant experience

Understanding what motivates your dream client enables you to organize and showcase your experiences more effectively. Your work is as good as your work can be, and this book will not change that. What it will do, though, is help you to present your experience and past work in such a way that it gives your dream client the assurances they need, and you the best possible chance of achieving a perceived value that supports the financial objectives you're looking to achieve.

Understanding framing & messaging

Joshua Bell is a world-renowned violinist and former musical child prodigy who regularly sells out concert halls at $100 per seat with his virtuoso performances.

He commands such attention primarily due to his skills, but he also has a carefully crafted image to thank. This "framing" of Joshua and what he does; the reputation and glamour of a world-class musical experience; the taste, feel, surroundings of an electric atmosphere and cultivated online presence; are all catalysts for justifying this cost.

The marketing of these events echoes this. Post-sale, everything – from the presentation of the tickets, the dress code, prohibitive pricing points, valet parking and premium service – defines this as a *potentially life-changing* product.

Still, **at his core, Joshua is a musician** – a musician who has been brilliantly "packaged" or 'framed' as a premium product.

So what happens if you remove the frame?

The *Washington Post* decided to carry out a study, which ***removed everything about Joshua's performance but the music***. They placed a plainly clad Joshua and his violin in a DC Metro station, and asked him to play exactly the same pieces he had performed the previous night to a packed Orchestral Hall.

You can probably guess what happened next. The study allowed a similar number of people (1097) to walk past the busking Joshua as had seen him the previous night at $100 a ticket. A grand total of seven people stopped to pay him any sort of attention. The same scintillating performance from the previous night – minus the messaging and associated framing – garnered a grand total of $32 and change in the street environment.

The core "product" (the performance) was exactly the same, yet the framing and messaging provided a much different outcome in terms of revenue.

I hope this serves to illustrate my point. Your audience may be passing you by because they can't relate to your service enough to *really desire it.*

As we described earlier in the book, if you just 'specialize in building websites' you're just another musician on the subway ride home who might get lucky. Contrast that with what might happen if you wrap what you do into something that makes an impact, and builds connection and desire. That's right: **you'll** be the one attracting the standing ovation.

When thinking about how to apply this to your own business, you should start by understanding that messaging and framing can best be described as 'providing an experience'. At its most basic level, a Ferrari F430 is a 'mode of transport'. No different than a bus, a bicycle or a beat-up old Nissan.

Do you think that's the way it's sold? Nope. Owning a vehicle like this increases prestige, demonstrates success, enhances perceived attractiveness and wealth. These are crucial *emotional triggers* played upon within any Ferrari marketing activity.

When you purchase a Ferrari, you're not just buying into a vehicle. You're buying into a lifestyle – and an exclusive one at that.

So how can you make your prospects buy in to the experience of what you're doing?

The product will essentially remain the same. But you need to describe the experiential outcome. You need to crank up the contrast between the client's life with you as their service provider, and life without you.

This may seem a little drastic, and these examples are extreme to help you understand it. In truth, if you're a freelance copywriter, for example, I don't expect your product to change your clients entire take on life. However, doesn't it make sense to understand what they desire and position your service to speak to those sensitivities?

You need to talk to *'Sam'*.

Are you resonating with 'Sam'?

D Bnonn Tennant (yes, real name) is an authority in the field of copywriting for conversion. The interview I held with him on a cold Thursday night (10 a.m. the next day for him, being a Kiwi) was a joy to be part of. We started by trying to pin down why it is that freelancers struggle with building out a useful web presence, one that delivers leads and grows their business.

"The thing is, in school we're taught that writing is hard, but it isn't. You just need to write like you talk," he said, and I hung on for how he'd continue.

*"So rather than sitting down trying to **write** for a built-up, abstract idea of an ideal prospect, imagine it's a person and you're sitting across from them, just **talking**. Call them 'Sam', to make it personal."*

"What are you going to say verbally to Sam, given what he's currently thinking? Then what are you going to follow that up with to get him to stick around?"

— D Bnonn Tennant on Freelancelift Q&A

In those 88 words, he articulated what it generally takes me an hour to hammer home: that ultimately, clients come to you hoping *to solve a problem they have*. Nothing more, nothing less. Your skills — they expect — are the vehicle for getting from their current situation to where they want to be. But it isn't the skills they really care about.

If you did meet Sam, face-to-face, would you start your conversation (imagining he'd already laid out his problems to you) by launching into a story about how great you are at Photoshop? Or would you genuinely tell someone to their face that you 'specialize in building websites'?

Probably not. You'd empathize, relate and ultimately position yourself as someone who has solved that problem for others before, then give him some pointers as to what steps he should take from here.

On another Q&A call, Robert Williams, a designer and founder at letsworkshop.com, had a similar message.

"A common thread I hear from freelancers is that once they get a prospect on a Skype call or face to face, it becomes easy to get them to be a client. But they find it really difficult to get them from their website or email, to talking in person."

"To which I say, 'so what are you not saying in your copy, that you're saying in person?"

- Robert Williams on Freelancelift Q&A

This is a great point. If a client lands with you and is immediately hit with a vague headline, buzzwords and descriptions of the software you're great at using (but which they've never heard of), it's a fundamentally different experience to the one they'll get if you meet them in a coffee shop.

In that informal setting, you'd cater your language to suit their experience level, and simplify your message so that it resonated with them and their issues.

So what are the sensitivities of your dream client, and how can you tailor your messaging towards that?

Who is your dream client and what motivates them?

It's easy to get bogged down by various blog posts and conflicting advice around understanding your 'buyer persona' or 'target demographic'. As with most things, all it does is give us an excuse for procrastination. "Ah well, I can't do XYZ yet because I need to research my buyer persona first."

In your *one-page of intent,* you mapped out the worldview of the target you were looking to speak to.

In this section, we'll add to that with some basic questions, but I implore you not to get stuck on this section. The point is to make assumptions (if needed) to get going, then continually iterate and evolve the picture of your ideal client. This book centers around evolution, of constantly learning and improving. The same applies to the concept of **who,** specifically, you're looking to work with.

I've listed five simple questions to help you pin down a dream client we can work towards. These should form part of every pre-sales discussion, too, to give you a quick barometer.

1. What do they care about most?

What are their virtues and values? Do they value time, money, happiness, belonging? What drives them on a personal level?

Example (back to the web design for musicians example): They have underlying ambitions they feel are not met yet, so while they do have an element of striving for money, their drive is ultimately a pursuit of a platform and freedom – and of being adored.

2. What positive qualities do they carry?

Every client should have positive qualities to bring to the table. Bad apples will not display these or will only showcase negatives. Are they passionate about their craft? Driven? Motivated to do more? Super-friendly? Well-connected? Generous?

Example: They have passion that can be felt instantly, with general happiness that makes the relationship much easier; patience; and professionalism that will ensure things are handled diligently.

3. How clear is their vision?

Will they allow you to flex your expertise and imagination to help them reach their goal, or will they stifle your creativity by having pre-conceived ideas?

Example: They do have clear goals, but concede that they have to invest in talent to make that happen. They're prepared to give creative freedom for new ideas in the pursuit of this goal.

4. What is their financial outlook?

If you are going to make more money every month, you need to work with financially liquid clients. This should not be confused with wealth, though. Some wealthy clients are a pain and barter over every penny, while others will pour their life into investing at the very limits of their capability for the right project.

Example: They currently generate over $5,000 per month in revenue from various activities. This ensures that my target project value ($4,000) is within their reach, given that the asset will work for their business for 2 years or more.

5. In real terms, what do they expect working with you to deliver?

When scoping out a client and project, you should have clear areas you can make an impact on. When you spell out the upside, specifically, and get the client's buy-in, it makes justifying a cost almost trivial. If you have a clear objective the client believes you can achieve, you have the freedom to build a fee that's weighted against this upside.

Example: The client understands that a new website would give them the ability increase conversion levels for ticket and .mp3 sales by a factor of 10%-50%, potentially unlocking revenues that are currently being left on the table. In doing so, they'll be able to recoup their investment quickly. The secondary benefit would be a more modern web presence that would attract the interest of larger record labels.

By answering these five simple questions, you can begin to build a picture of who 'Sam' is and what his sensitivities are. We can use this insight (along with everything from our *one-page of intent*) to build a message, which attracts and retains the interest of a dream client.

Before we do that, its important to understand **why** clients are looking for your service in the first place. This key driver will provide the context for all of your messaging.

Pain comes before any action

Pain (noun): a feeling of distress, suffering, or agony

We're all familiar with the feeling of minor pain. This is a protective mechanism in the human nervous system that stimulates a reaction. If something is hot to the touch, pain receptors trigger the reflex action that causes us to drop the hot object before it burns our fingers.

Businesses have pain receptors, too. In most cases, it is this pain that creates the environment for research and action.

Indeed, a nagging pain is generally a signal that something deeper is wrong. The mistake most freelancers make is to ignore the fact that opportunities to make a sale are only made possible by a business pain.

With access to information easier than ever, business pain tends to lead to research and investigation into the problem. As this research deepens, a client gains an ability to confidently articulate the remedy they feel they require. It is a huge mistake to take this self-diagnosis at face value and assume that the prospect actually understands what they need.

Here's an example of how this process works, from pain to action from the perspective of your would-be client (using the case of a web designer):

Pain
- Bob (the customer) told me he couldn't access our website on his mobile, so we lost the deal.

Research
- I asked Jane, who looks at our site stats, and mentioned that our bounce rate is really high
- I did some research and found that my site isn't equipped to deal with mobiles and tablets – maybe I need a mobile website!
- I did more research and now understand that a mobile site isn't great for search engines. Having a responsive website is better.

Action
-        I need a web designer to create a more responsive website for me.

This is a perfectly normal scenario. Yet at this point, most freelancers are speaking with the prospect in the language of *responsive design* (they are serving the prospect's request, after all) and not the language of **pain** (the initial driver of the request).

It's the difference between talking to the prospect about:

The benefits of valid HTML5 menu items in responsive design
They might nod along and say, "Oh, okay, that's interesting." But it won't necessarily inspire them to see you as the only solution to their problems.

Vs.

How many 'Bobs' are you losing every day? A lot, right? Well, I've made lots of sites like yours 'Bob-friendly.'

By focusing on the pain so that it makes its root cause crystal clear – and in language that makes sense to the prospect's worldview – you build authority, connection and make it easy to align their objectives with your service.

Take a look at the underlying pains at play in your space. What research track could a prospect find themselves on, and how can you position your service to speak to the pain rather than the remedy?

This activity will be the crux of mapping out your brand message.

Your difference statement

The purpose of this book is to provide you with ideas and actionable points without detracting from your day-to-day activity. One of the biggest and most impactful moves you can make in business is to develop a 'difference statement'. A simple, punchy paragraph that gives an anchor point for your brand and will influence later decisions.

We've already mapped out your specialty, a prospect's worldview, and their primary drivers. Now it's about pulling those elements together into something that resonates with that dream client, and which you can relate to the rest of your site content and brand touchpoints.

Without a dependable core message, you'll find it difficult to think through some problems strategically. Should I take on that client? Would it work for me to be advertised in this space? Shall I go to that industry conference?

If you can cross-reference decisions like that using your difference statement (which lays out your vision and what you stand for), you can be sure you'll invest time and energy in the activities and projects that really matter.

A basic formula

The formula for this statement is fairly basic, and deliberately so as it should be easy to create and adapt over time.

[brandname] [standfor]. We help [customer] by [the frame] with [primary] and [secondary]

This simple paragraph, in less than 100 words, gives you something for your brand to look towards.

[customer] The specialized sector we identified in the one-page of intent.
[primary, secondary] Defines and documents your primary and secondary product set.

[standfor] Pick your end of the market and define what you stand for.
[theframe] What's the frame for your product/service?

Let's look at these one by one.

Customer

In the first phase we explained the purpose of a specific, targeted, smaller pool of prospective clients. Then we looked at defining that dream client, and painting a picture of their worldview. You have the opportunity at this point to wrap that sense of 'Sam' into a coherent label.

With Freelancelift, I'm not just targeting "small businesses." I'm specifically targeting freelance designers, writers and marketers.

Sure, there may be some people who join us for the ride. But for your core message to resonate, you must be specific.

Example: "Freelance designers, writers & marketers"

Primary & Secondary product

Defining these is another crucial point. Again, it all sounds kind of obvious, but it just doesn't happen a lot of the time. So, first of all, what is your primary product or service?

You're a web designer, sure, and most people get that. Now then, what about a secondary service? This is where you need to start to think like a bigger business and lose the freelance blinkers.

You may have at least three secondary services for every one primary service. This will form the basis for your income stability plans when we get to Phase IV.

Example:

Primary – No Bullshit business growth ideas
Secondary – Genius Q&A Calls, Playbooks & Video Training

What you stand for

Here's where you may start to exit your comfort zone. What do you stand for? Think about that for a second. Are you a boutique service, where quality and attention to detail is paramount? Or are you going for volume purchases in the lower ranges?

Both have their advantages and disadvantages, but you can't afford to sit on the fence. If you find yourself with bad-apple clients, you probably have a problem with your positioning. Doing it right – positioning yourself where you're most effective – will help protect against attracting the wrong type of client.

Put it in the context of your dream client. How can you articulate your values in a language that connects with the worldview and sensitivities of your dream client?

The great part is that bad apples won't care what you stand for. They just want it cheaper, faster and will hire a laborer. Your core messaging (in their eyes, vague BS) will distract them, maybe even offend them, and ultimately repel them from reaching out to you.

Dream clients will connect with your mission to improve their business holistically. They understand that this takes time, and that they should lean on your expertise in a genuine partnership.

I strive to help freelancers grow, to provide something that wasn't available to me in my first stint as a freelancer.

Example: I strive to help freelancers earn more this month than they did last month, by leveraging big-business thinking and creating a state of constant evolutionary improvement.

The frame

We discussed earlier how a frame – a sense of value – can give you a license to bill considerably more. Whether it's for a BMW dressed up as a Rolls Royce or a world-class musician dressed as a busker, "framing" has the ability to dramatically increase or decrease your perceived value to prospects.

A bad pitch or bad client reaction to a proposal price is almost always connected to poor framing or badly positioned messaging. It usually has nothing to do with your ability as a freelancer.

Put into words how you improve the lives of your clients. Try to do it without mentioning your primary or secondary service.

Example: I provide the confidence that comes from income stability and business predictability.

Bringing it all together

[companyname] [standfor]. We help [customer] by [theframe] with [primary] and [secondary]

So here's how mine comes together:

"Freelancelift exists to help freelancers earn more this month than they did last month, by leveraging big-business thinking and creating a state of constant evolutionary improvement.

We provide you with the confidence that comes from income stability and business predictability with our no-bullshit business growth ideas, Genius Q&A Calls, Playbooks & Video training."

The key here is to use this powerful statement to your advantage. Place it at the heart of your marketing and your sales processes. Use it to guide headlines, website copy and online profiles.

This statement should be the essence of your brand – something you can adapt to differing environments to build consistency and clarity of message.

Putting messaging into practice

With this refined idea of your business outlook, you should put your messaging to work, starting with your website content.

The point of creating website copy is to allow your dream client to quickly understand that you can solve the problem they have. More often than not, you'll have only a few seconds to get this message across.

Your copy should contain an implied promise, backed by a deep understanding of the pain being experienced by the prospect at that point.

Your **headline** should attract and connect, your **body** copy should empathize and persuade, and your **call to action** should spell out the specific action you'd like them to take next.

This is copywriting at its most basic, and it doesn't need to get more technical than that. Here are some prompters you can use to create messaging that works with your goals, rather than against them.

Leverage an effective headline

It is important to consider that if your website's job is to convert an otherwise passive visitor into something of value to your business, you need to ensure that visitors will engage with your message quickly.

Fewer than 25% of web visitors continue to the body copy after reading the headline on any given page. That's huge. If you can improve your site's 'stickiness' by using impactful, relevant headlines, you'll have a much higher likelihood of having the visitor engage with you and your message.

If the objective of the website initially is to demand attention, then you could do worse than ensuring your headlines are fit for the purpose. Make a promise, a specific reason to stick around. Now write it down in 10 words or less.

Tell them why they're in this situation

If you can explain someone's problem or situation better than they can, you'll develop instant credibility. This ability only comes from getting inside the minds of your dream client (and after you've gone through the exercises laid out in this phase).

First, you should be able to gain their interest and trust. Then follow that up with structured advice, just as if you were sitting across from them in a coffee shop.

Show them your passion

Use descriptive language to "show" (rather than tell) how you've seen their scenario before, and how you reversed it. Use a story of connection to cement that trust. Emphasize how you're passionate about solving that problem and how you've done so before. Video is particularly useful here, as it's significantly easier to display your passion and empathy.

Use contrast, transform

It's important to crank up the contrast. What does life look like with you as a business partner, as opposed to life without you?

What will happen if they don't make changes quickly? You can exaggerate the current position and transform those pain points by showing them how you can help them transform their status quo.

Explain the solution

You should be able to explain the benefits and the upside of your solution, not the features, nuts and bolts. If you relate these benefits back to the pain, worldview and key motivators of your dream client, you'll be able to show in a concrete way why your product is a must for your prospect.

Modeling

Use stories when defining your frame. Ideally, you'll have other success stories to call upon. Your prospects can model themselves on these success stories.

Providing an "if they've done it for them, they can do it for me" moment (especially with solid proof) is a great way to enhance the prospect's *belief* in the capabilities of your product or service.

Maximise the value

Especially in an online situation, you should be provide value in your space. This is a key takeaway from Phase III. For now, though, just remember that if you can teach your prospects in a way that doesn't feel like a sales pitch, you'll maximise their trust and connection with your message.

Own the pre-sales conversation with a 'need not apply' list

There are few things more powerful than arguing against your own cause when it comes to persuasion. You're in business, a service provider, so it stands to reason that you're going to be doing everything in your power to persuade otherwise passive visitors to get in touch, buy your service, send you an email, and so on.

What that visitor is not expecting is a list of reasons **why they should not.**

Put simply, if you're able to say clearly, maturely:

"I work best with [insert dream client characteristics], if you're looking for quick results for the lowest cost, or for someone to simply take your instructions I don't think we'll be a good fit for each other."

If you know what the early warning signs are for good and bad clients, you can repel potentially bad clients by convincing them that they 'need not apply'.

You don't need to put it in negative terms, either. This technique works for simply extending any touchpoints on your site or onboarding process so that you allow prospective clients to self-select which 'bucket' they fall into.

Reach for the stars

Your copy and framing should point to the 'victory'. We have a clear understanding of what your dream client wants, so make sure that you paint a picture of what victory looks like. By doing so throughout your copy, you'll continually be able to persuade and edge your prospect along.

Call to action

It goes without saying that you should have a clear call to action. It should cover how easy it is to get started, give them a no-brainer way to start the relationship, and bring them into the loop of what the process will looks like from that point on.

At this point, you can also use contrast as a tool. Spell out what *not taking action looks* like.

Build out more effective brand touchpoints

What most us envisage when we hear the word 'branding' is a logo, website or a USP. Don't confuse brand with design. The truth is these are the just the 'front men' of your brand – they serve to bring something tangible to the intangible 'aura' of you and your business.

A *brand* goes much deeper. It's what a prospect *feels* when they receive an email from you. It's the impression you leave when they speak to you on the phone, and what they take away from your website copy or blog.

Consider your core message, design and other touchpoints as the embodiment of your brand. They should be consistent and support your difference statement.

A great brand punches through every time a prospective or current client has any exposure to your business. These 'touchpoints' should leave the best possible impression on the types of people you want to resonate with.

So your website, emails, social profiles, portfolio, proposals, pitches should all align to give a consistent experience, one that bolsters your potential to make a sale.

In this section, we'll look at these brand touchpoints. Perfecting these will provide you with a much greater sense of 'brand'. When these brand touchpoints influence perception of value, and when perception influences the cost you can justifiably bill, it pays to get them right.

What's in a name?

My objective with this book (and with everything I teach at Freelancelift) is to provide the highest-leverage changes to your business. To that end, it's rare for me to talk about *brand names,* as this topic often confuses freelancers and the debate only prolongs procrastination. For me, this is an 'icing' issue, rather than the cake itself.

On the whole, I see no dramatic increase in freelancer success when I compare those working under a named brand (arelevantbrand.com) with those operating under their own name (yourname.com).

Sure, a brand name can have a multiplier effect, but it's something to consider once you have established a business infrastructure destined for growth.

So does it matter?

For me the answer is, It Depends.

If you're looking to build a business that has the potential to exist and grow without you in it, then a named brand can help. (This is what I wanted to achieve with Tone, hence the name 'Tone', not 'Liam.').

If you have a specific audience and you're able to build a brand name that tells your story and resonates quickly, or if this is a side-project for a more specific audience, then a brand name can assist with that, too (this was true with Freelancelift).

Finally, if you want to gain traction by using a short, memorable domain name with wider-ranging benefits, a branded name can help (Hence tone.co.uk).

My experiences with using brand names (instead of my own name) have been good, but I don't count them as crucial ingredients. That's why I provide no recommendations either way.

That said, in some ways a brand name is impersonal. It can be difficult to tell your story through it, or to provide depth of voice.

It can also create challenges on social media. In that arena, you might have no presence (if you're operating just one account, under the brand name), or you may duplicate effort when you also maintain a personal brand.

Paul Jarvis (pjrvs.com), who I interviewed in the run-up to this book, has a very successful design business under his own moniker. So do Sacha Greif, Nathan Barry and others.

That's because they got the underlying fundamentals of their business right. They experienced success because of *that*, not because of what they named their primary service business.

Commit to good design practice

So although your brand isn't *just design*, there is no getting away from the fact that your brand is, more often than not, *brought to life through design*.

I find it frustrating when I see good freelancers with a poor brand. The most obvious place for poor branding to manifest itself is in shoddily designed brand touchpoints. Some might argue that design doesn't matter, or that good design is subjective. In some cases I agree. But, more than anything, what you need to have in place is **good design practice.**

A website that brings your message to life

What you need to understand is that there are websites, and there are *websites that work*. The two are very different. Allow me to explain.

You might already have a website, but if it isn't contributing to leads, sales and your wider online reputation, it *isn't working*.

You should be clear that your web presence anchors the rest of your online reputation. It should act as **its steward** by drawing in visits from other locations on the web and directing them to complete something of value to your business.

Depending on who you listen to, the design of your site is either crucial or irrelevant. My particular take is that a clean, simple design – one equipped for the rigors of modern web browsing habits, and which gives your messaging center stage – is **crucial**. One of my pet hates is poor design, because there's simply no excuse for it.

With a platform like Squarespace you can create simple, effective and beautiful looking websites in less than an hour.

Or you could head to Themeforest.com and pick up a world-class theme for under $50. The tools are out there, so don't deliberate too much over it.

You should ensure that your design is modern, clean, and interesting. And if you're not a designer, don't try to be one. Design should not take away from the primary goals of your site and should not upstage your core message.

It's essential that your site is responsive, too. The increase in mobile and tablet browsing in recent times is huge, so responsiveness is now pretty much a pre-requisite.

Kick-ass proposals & the art of pitching

When it comes to advising freelancers on creating proposals, a huge majority of information in the freelancer blog space falls significantly wide of the mark.

You'll find an abundance of proposal templates, structure guides and accompanying hot air. The people putting these out there have good intentions, but ultimately those tools fail to deliver.

Chances are that you'll conduct 80% of your business over email, Skype or telephone, so you don't really need to know about salesmanship, right?

Wrong!

The medium might be different, but the process is as old as the hills:

> Step 1. Party A has a need for goods that Party B can provide
> Step 2. Party B explains the features and benefits of the goods
> Step 3. Party B offers a price
> Step 4. The parties negotiate
> Step 5. A mutually agreeable price is determined
> Step 6. Goods exchange is completed

This is the same process for a freelancer selling web services in 2015 AD, and a market trader in Ancient Egypt bartering for cloth in 2015 BC.

Remember, you can improve, optimize and maximize every link in that six-step chain. When you realize you're not exempt from 'selling' as an art, you can begin to understand what it takes to make more revenue per client and win more clients to begin with.

Billing on value provided, not time spent

If you're billing on the value you provide, time should no longer be a factor. You should bill for the completion of a project, on a fixed-fee basis. If that project is inherently time-related (an ongoing marketing campaign, for example) you should bill based on a significant chunk of time (so the 'project' in this instance would be the next quarter of activity).

Remember, the price a client is comfortable paying is directly related to the value they feel they're going to get from it. You control this perceived value in the messaging and touchpoints you put in front of your prospects. Somake these touchpoints pay.

The value of discovery

If you take the time to truly understand your prospect's space and current situation, you'll have the inside track on what makes them tick, what an average customer is worth and how your work will make an impact. You have the ability to speak to their sensitivities and a much greater chance of developing a longer-term relationship.

By understanding deeply what a client is looking to achieve from a project, you can attach monetary figures to the upside your work will bring.

I advocate switching sides of the desk. Start looking at your pricing from the point of view of your client.

This helps for two reasons. It allows you to fine-tune your messaging so that there is no element of doubt in your client's mind that you are the right person for this job. More importantly, it helps give you clarity on the cost/benefit decision your client will have to make.

Know your prospect's market intimately. If you do have the opportunity to scope out the project before drafting your the proposal, try to get as much detail as you can about the upside your client expects from this new project. Some great questions to ask are:

- What is your average customer worth?
- Will this logo/website/application/ebook/content make it easier for you to get clients?
- Will this save you time? How much?

- What does success look like to you?
- What is holding you back from hitting your current targets?

Leveraging these techniques will give you the comfort you need to justify in your own mind the basis for your new pricing structure. It also provide you with ammunition you can build into your messaging when you create your proposal.

Moreover, you'll build a sense of collaboration and trust between you and your prospective client.

The qualities of a great pitch

Even if you conduct all your proposal exchanges, pitches, negotiations and contracting online, you should not exclude yourself from understanding the qualities of a great proposal & pitch.

Get to the point

You should be able to wrap up any pitch in 20 minutes, so a proposal should be no longer than 6 pages of content (this will be longer if you include graphics). That might feel light, but think of your client – do they really want to work through 30 pages of text? Or would they be happy to receive something shorter that still addresses all of their concerns?

Tell me something I don't know

In human psychology, we tend to block out information we think we already know. It's a natural protection against absorbing too much useless information. So, in a proposal or pitch situation, lead with something intriguing. An idea, a statistic, killer research or something simply unexpected that ensures that the prospect will sit up and listen.

It's all about me

Unfortunately, clients do not care a whole lot about you. Sure, they need to understand that you're a great person, easy to get along with and have the skills to do the job. They don't need to know what software you're skilled in using, though, or which high school you went to (unless it specifically relates to them and achieving their goals).

Remember, clients don't hire you because you can design/code/write. They hire you because they believe you can solve a problem in their business.

Pace the problem

In a similar way, your prospect doesn't really care about the features or technical details of your proposal. Yes, they need to be in there, but ensure they're described in a section that follows the pricing.

They need to know you understand their problem, 'pacing' is a storytelling technique where you put in the work to describe their problem so clearly and vividly that they can almost imagine themselves pacing up and down, in their own mind trying to solve it.

Understand what it is they really desire from investing in this project, and leave no doubt in your pitch or proposal that your solution will solve this problem easily, efficiently and conclusively.

Show me the upside

If you're going to be asking for anything significant from a client, you should be looking to justify that spend against the likely upside. Given you've already told them how investing in you will solve their problem, what does that mean to them financially, and why does that make your asking price a no-brainer?

An efficient proposal structure

When drafting a value-based pitch or proposal, you only need to do three things:

1. Build value
2. Justify the investment & upside
3. Ask for the sale

Adapt to your own needs, but here is an example structure to follow:

Building value

Section 1: Pace the problem
Does your prospect have a problem getting new customers? Are they suffering from a shortage of time? Whatever their main pain is, in this section you need to run through it to demonstrate that you intimately understand their problem. What impact is it having on their business right now? What does this pain cause them not to do?

Section 2: Echo worldview and main sensitivities
There are several reasons clients why won't buy, but often it's simply because you're not addressing their primary concerns. What beliefs do they have about how you can help? What are their fears about getting this decision wrong? You should build empathy in this section by making it clear you're fully on board with what they're trying to achieve. Have a counter-argument for each potential objection spelled out.

Section 3: Make them believe you
In this section, leave no doubt in the prospect's mind that you can walk the walk as well as you talk the talk. Here is where you can discuss successes you've had with similar projects, your reputation within the space, and how this directly relates to the work you're pitching to win for the prospect.

Section 4: Make them value you
Stories often are the best way to put points across; moreover, they builds trust and empathy that is difficult to replicate using other means. We've discussed

how clients primarily care about their own pains and remedying those, but that shouldn't stop you talking about your journey and relating any story about your background to the prospect and their particular problem. Your objective here is to make the prospect *value* the impact you, specifically, would bring to this project.

Section 5: Provide the details

It wouldn't be a proposal without some finer points. At this point, if you're in the web business, it'll be the technical aspects. Otherwise, just be clear about what the prospect will get in return and what they will not.

Justify the investment & upside

Section 6: What does victory look like?

If your prospect cannot clearly visualize the successful finish you're going to bring them to, it will be difficult to keep them engaged with your proposal or pitch. At this point, we're building up to the price reveal, so it's important to ramp up the excitement.

Ultimately a prospect has a subconscious eye on 'what difference will this make to me?' 'Why will this make my life better?'

Your job here is to answer those questions, respond strongly, and begin to justify the investment.

Section 7: What is the upside?

Now we're getting into specifics. Sure, quality of life is an important factor, but we need to facilitate a rational decision-making process by spelling out the financial upside. You can look as far into the future as you need to here (depending on the service you're carrying out).

You may express the upside as a month-to-month figure (e.g., "By doing XYZ, you save around $1k per month in rescued productivity"), or you might want to justify your investment as a longer-term play (e.g,. "By redeveloping the site and upping the conversion rate to 3%, you'll be in a position to generate an additional $100k over the next 12 months").

Pick whichever method suits your payment structure and the natural duration of the investment. If you don't feel comfortable quoting precise figures, or you haven't been able to gather enough specific information, you should spell out the beneficial factors here in terms of business growth, brand awareness, more sales or saved time. Allow your prospect to connect the dots in terms of what the value of that is to them.

You will have a 'sense' of what this upside is yourself, but if you don't feel comfortable putting it down, you can leave it out. Just make sure that this sense forms the basis of your pricing.

Section 8: What is the investment?

Here is where you pitch your cost. If you've done everything right to this point, the price should be trivial a trivial consideration for the prospect. Providing that you have fully justified the value you bring to the table and the investment is proportionally fair to the upside, you'll have a great chance of making the deal.

Ask for the sale

Section 9: Make it easy to say yes

Even if your service does not lend itself to a 'quick start' option, you should still look to make the final decision-making process simple and easy to agree on.

Sure, you'll probably need to have a *project initiation meeting*. Sure, you may need to *get content* or more information before you start (to be *set up with an email address,* or to review terms and conditions). But try to steer clear of mentioning this for now.

By adding unnecessary complexity to 'saying yes', you add distractions. You don't want them to day, "Oh shoot, John from tech is on holiday for two weeks. If you need that email address, maybe we'll need to hold off til he's back."

Just get the commitment first, and deal with the obligatory onboarding bits later.

Section 10: Assume the sale

This is Sales 101 stuff, but it's high on sales training lists because it works. If you can lead your prospect down a path to the extent that psychologically they've already committed, you control the closing process.

Example: "So, upon signature I will issue the first 50% invoice that covers everything up to when we launch. That's when the other 50% is due and you're completely happy – who would I address that first invoice to?"

You'll find your prospect clambering for a name rather than saying, "Hang on a minute, I haven't hired you yet."

To be clear, each one of these sections doesn't need to be horrendously long, nor do they need to add anything more to your current sales process. Proposals are often put together more for the benefit of the freelancer than the client. The objective of a value-stacked proposal like the one I've laid out is to reverse that. The proposal should speak the language of the client and support their decision to hire you.

Understand and improve your onboarding process

'Onboarding' can best be described as gradually introducing a person into a specific relationship or situation via a set of *induction actions*. If you've ever started a new job, you'll recall how effective your employer was at welcoming you into the team. If you've invested in new software, you'll have gone through a series of emails or on-page walkthroughs, which introduced you to key product features and generally got you up to speed.

But how does this apply to service businesses?

Whether you are aware of it or not, you already have an onboarding process. After you receive the signed order or the email that says 'Yes, let's do it!' onboarding includes every step that takes place from there, until such time as the client receives the first batch of work.

"Ensuring everyone is on the same page is critical to a successful partnership. Effective communication begins with careful listening with intent. How well are you communicating with your clients?"

                 - Shawn Hesketh, founder of WP101 on the Freelancelift Q&A

By not managing expectations, you're leaving the door open for bad apples. Here are the questions that will likely come up during the early stages of a relationship. If you can pre-package answers to these questions, you'll mold a client to the way *you* want to do business, not the way they want to.

- Who is working on my project and who do I contact day-to-day?
- Can I give you my suggestions up front? If so, how?
- How often will I hear from you?
- How will you update me on progress?
- What is the best method of communication?

At Tone we build websites (predominantly) and have a relatively simple, but effective onboarding process for new clients:

1. Discovery survey
    a. Client fills out an online survey (built with Typeform)
    b. This asks probing questions which require some thought on the part of the client to answer
2. Onboarding / welcome call
    a. Walk through the project management system
    b. Introduce project manager
    c. Describe communication channels
    d. Lay out timeline
    e. Review specifications
    f. Cover off 'scope creep'
3. Project initiation workshop
    a. Introduce project team
    b. Understand the client's business deeply
    c. Who is their dream client?
    d. Review discovery form responses
    e. Review key objectives and agree on what constitutes success
    f. Develop initial ideas based on the intersection of these objectives and our pre-conceived ideas
4. User journey and site structure
    a. Now that we know what the client's goals are and who their audience is, how will we structure the website so it enables their visitors to achieve these goals most efficiently
    b. How many pages does this require, what will go on each and how should they move from page to page?

At this point, the client is completely inducted into our way of doing things, is clear what's expected of them, the team is engaged with the project, and we can proceed in earnest. Onboarding gives everybody that clarity to start a project with gusto.

Working to a clear specification

One of the most common questions I'm asked is:

"I have a client, they're really pushy and want XYZ, but I thought I was only delivering X. We're quite a way into the project now and I want to keep them as a client, so I figure I'll have to do the XYZ but it's going to take me twice as long. How do I deal with this?"

More often than not, at that stage it's too late to 'deal with'. You're already past the point of no return. So you either walk away, lose a client and lose the earnings from the time you've already spent, or suck it up and do the XYZ. (I'll leave you to guess which route is more common!)

How do I prevent this?

Well, it starts with a clear specification. If you go to a builder with a set of architectural plans, what you'll receive back is an extensive quote with a list of costs for every single brick and each man-hour to be spent on the job.

This is a clear, precise, agreeable specification of the expected, agreed-upon work to be delivered. The word 'expected' here is deliberate, and I'll explain why.

When you see in the news "Building project goes over budget by $10m", you could be forgiven for thinking, "Well, you gave a price, how could it go over budget?"

Put simply, this happens when there is a miscalculation on the part of the client. The architect's drawings were not comprehensive enough, or the materials were more expensive than anticipated.

In a freelancer context, this is 'scope creep.' Unlike the freelancer, the builder does not take this on the chin. They simply bill more as required for this extension of the specification.

If you make it clear what you *expect* to complete, when it will be complete, and what each and every feature is supposed to look like, you'll have a watertight agreement you can refer back to.

If an element is not covered, it's a simple 'Sure, we can do that – but it will need to be added to the next phase'. (There is a caveat here, which we will discuss in Phase IV.) Sometimes it pays to over-deliver and not bill extra when you're hoping to build a longer-term partnership. Still, ensure that you have a solid specification to work to so that it's down to you to make that choice.

Don't diminish your earnings just because of a grey area or oversight in your onboarding and communication!

Relevant experience

The final element that influences a client's perception of you is the experience you have. This will have been made abundantly clear in your messaging, but at some point you're going to need to prove it.

By repositioning your website so that you're implementing design best practice you're going to make it easy for a client to digest what it is you're trying to say and to make their way into unearthing what experiences and prior work you're bringing to the table.

You may be in the fortunate position to have household names – within your specialized space - among your client roster. If you do, you should shout about this but if – like most – you're not quite at that level yet, what can you do?

You need to figure out what prospects are looking for when they absorb information about the projects you've completed before.

Pretty pictures help but what really sets you apart is a short, punchy case study covering **how your work made a difference,** set against the backdrop of the prospective client's worldview and their core values (as highlighted when we mapped out the dream client).

Ensure they believe you

This applies whether you do business online, in person or whether at this point you're faced with a prospect on your website considering getting in touch. You should introduce trust indicators that put you in control of the conversation, leave nothing to chance and be open about your successes.

Here are some ideas:

Video testimonials

If you can, use video it's much easier for your prospect to identify with the human emotion within the testimonial. This is a killer technique.

Written testimonial with headshot
This is the next best thing, but for extra cayenne pepper include a link with the option to "don't take our word for it, contact this person yourself" for a verified response. You'll be surprised how few people will take this up, but the mere offer of a direct email to one of your customers is so powerful.

Social proof
An easy way to validate that you are the real deal is to check out your social standing online. If you are active in the community and have some solid social proof you're going to certify yourself as a provider of repute.

"Strength in numbers" is an idiom we're all familiar with. We're conditioned to follow the natural flow of things and move in packs. So when faced with a straight decision a prospective client will always pick the freelancer who has the most friends, the most connections, the most followers and the largest perceived reputation.

There is a sense of security in taking the path with the least potential for surprise. You should know that this 'social proof' can make or break your chances in a competitive pitch situation so its up to you to start making the moves which improve your overall standing online.

As featured in...
Sometimes it's difficult to see the wood for the trees as this technique is used so frequently but in certain tech situations it does carry some clout.

You'll build a more positive perception - when it comes to demonstrating relevant experience - by making bold, yet genuine claims as to the success you've achieved for other clients.

Then you should validate these claims with easily verified trust factors and give them as much visibility as possible within your website and sales processes.

Consider taking on free work to create the perfect portfolio

In my opinion this should be used sparingly, and be considered marketing rather than actual day-to-day work. It's something we will dive deep on in phase III but it warrants mentioning here; if you're new to an industry and want to build credibility by working with good clients and achieving great results consider taking the short-term hit on income for the longer term benefit of excellent value perception.

More on that in the next phase of the book.

Bad apple clients are grown, not inherited

Most of what you have just consumed may be new information but the entire message can be condensed for brevity into one succinct, 78 word paragraph.

It's up to you alone to paint a picture of your dream client. With this information you can engineer a perception of value and a core reason for being which will attract their attention and repel bad apples.

Framing this value in website messaging and backing it up with good discovery, effective communication and an excellent proposal will allow you to bill two or three times more than you do currently and keep over delivery to a minimum.

At this stage you will hopefully be committed to evolution and have a rock solid foundation of key objectives and core principles in place. This is the infrastructure that will ensure you are ready to convert attention into great clients.

In the next phase we will look to generate more of that attention, to multiply your exposure and build your platform.

Phase III

Multiply exposure and build your platform

Russia is a really difficult place to gain entry to. After a strenuous hour of shuffling through Moscow Domodedovo Airport immigration we finally made it into the arrivals lounge, my wife - then girlfriend - Michelle and me.

Jaded from the trip, we managed to spot our guide Igor from behind the barrier, accompanied by his friend and driver Vladimir. Igor clutched a sign with my name hastily scribbled in marker and with both carrying with stocky build and leather jackets they looked as Russian as their traditional names implied.

As we embraced and made our way out to the car park Vladimir looked us up and down with a chuckle, "you will be cold" he coughed. He wasn't wrong, we had wandered out into a sub-zero blizzard and the cold gripped my nose like a frozen clothes peg. Before that trip I thought Manchester was cold!

Igor was a promoter, he hosted numerous dance music events throughout Russia and Ukraine, and this was the evening before I was due to perform at his show.

At this point I was part designer – first time around - part musician (well, if pushing a few buttons to create electronic music counts) and had been booked to perform the headline DJ slot at an excellent Moscow venue.

This profession took me around the World over a crazy two years. From another brisk climate in Stockholm, Sweden to the dry heat of San Antonio, Ibiza and the effervescent climbs of Australia, where I toured the East Coast, playing in Sydney, Brisbane and Melbourne.

I'd been a DJ for years and considered myself fairly adept sure, but I was a young guy from the UK and barely the *best* – technically - in my home town, let alone my region, my country or the World. So, why me? Why would I be plucked from a foreign country to appear at Igor's event?

Put simply, I was doing what my fellow DJs and musicians were not, I was **providing value** in the space and I'd built an online platform which allowed me to broadcast that value without international boundaries.

I had committed to *putting out content* from my own original music (Look me up on Spotify) to the monthly podcast I released. I set up a record label for new artists, I hosted events and competitions, I taught what I knew via video tutorials and in general was *just active.* I was as involved in the industry as I could be and didn't lock myself away bemoaning my lack of a 'big break' looking for the next X-Factor auditions.

As a freelancer you face the same issues as those faced by the music community. There are thousands, if not millions of your fellow freelancers fighting for that same *headline slot.* That dream client. Are you going to be the 'bedroom DJ' freelancer who battles hard, treads water but ultimately fails to push forward with anything other than lower quality clients and a scraped living? Or will you take the steps required to **demand** attention in this sea of voices? Our objective for this phase of the book is to build attention, the right sort of attention at that.

What is attention anyway?

We live in a noisy world. Whether it's the irresistibly tactile Facebook notification icon or the audible blip of your email client, everybody wants a piece of your attention.

The same is true for your prospective client. Their time is limited and ability to pay attention *severely* exhausted. This is compounded by the fact that there have never been so many easy ways to seek answers for the pains and problems they have (that your service would ultimately remedy).

This makes for a cloudy online environment and your dream client has developed self-preserving defenses, which guard against advertising, information overload and general interruptions.

Most freelancers see this 'noise' as a barrier, "how the hell is anybody going to find me among this herd?" More often than not, this pushes them into channels like Elance or oDesk. "Well this should be more productive, people are *actually looking* for freelancers on here, right?"

This is flawed logic. We feel some comfort in the fact that potential clients are being attracted to this honeypot every day. We sense that at least we have a *chance* of making a sale here without actually understanding what type of sale we might make and more importantly, *to whom.*

You're voluntarily blending yourself into the herd, and in doing so procrastinating, putting out fires short term while holding off doing the longer term activities that will land you your dream client down the line. By treading water in freelancer exchanges you're willfully attracting bad apples.

My first time around as a freelancer I played the same mind games with myself, "hey this guy has earned like $900k this past 12 months on Elance I must be able to at least get a slice of that?"

What I neglected to inform my naive former self was that this was in fact a 60-person web development house based in India whose average project fee was $200.

Do you really want to take on 20 projects a month just to meet your financial goals?

I thought not.

So how do we multiply our exposure, build attention and look at this cloudy online environment as a *help* rather than hindrance?

How and when does your dream client go to market?

Some observers would call pre-Christmas hysteria harmless fun; others call it *relentless business.* In the cutthroat world of retail and consumer services *'visibility'* is a do or die word.

If you're anything like me, you'll feel it all comes around a bit too quickly. The summer sun fades and as we near the end of October the nights begin to draw shorter (a Northern Hemisphere vantage point if course).

Then without much warning, **bam'** the Christmas advertising begins. Most armchair marketers (on Twitter) might denounce this as crazy, too early or an unwelcome reminder of everything we'll need to arrange during that time.

The third sense aroused is intentional and deliberate, the other feelings questioning its efficacy are fundamentally incorrect and demonstrate a lack of understanding as to buying cycles.

The world of big business understands its *customer worldview and buying habits intimately*; their shareholders' pocket linings depend on it. It's no coincidence the big budget TV campaigns begin the first day of November.

So why does the ramp up start *so early*?

Put simply, it doesn't start early at all; the timing is perfect.

At this time of the year, an audience with buying intent begins going to market naturally. Even for the ones that do their Christmas shopping later (myself included), this attention and visibility begins to raise *thoughts of preparation,* which means my buying cycle is at least begun. These businesses are taking the steps to **own the conversation**, ensure their campaigns position them front of mind for their prospects, in order that they can engineer and influence a sales cycle.

Your advantage

Believe it or not you have several crucial advantages against your Megacorp cousins on two counts:

1. You can borrow their strategies without having to worry about fitting it all into a 4-6 week seasonal window.
2. You have a much more specific audience and easier access to the locations they hang out in.

Your service is - or should be - in demand all year round and now that we've humanized our dream client, mapped out their worldview, have laid out the pains they're experiencing and are clear on what they're *already trying* we have the insight required to own the pre-sales conversation for ourselves.

You can do all of this without investing in a primetime TV ad slot; in most cases you can own the conversation for no monetary cost at all.

Whether they know it or not, that exasperated Google query your dream client just made, having felt 'the pain' for the *'fifth time this week'* is **step one** on their buying journey.

A fundamental mistake (and something I'm hoping this book will allow you to understand) is the notion that a customer's buying cycle begins when they have a brief and know what they need.

That point is *much too late*, like starting your seasonal ad campaign on Christmas Eve. Your prospective client has already carried out enough research and been influenced by enough third parties to ensure you (as a newcomer to the party) would be significantly down the pecking order even if they haven't yet found a solution that fits.

This is another reason I don't recommend freelancer exchanges as viable long-term client channels. Would-be clients who appear on these channels have already carried out a significant amount of research as to what they need, more often than not finding the perfect supplier or solution already (yes you read that correctly)

There's just one problem, the perfect supplier or solution is much more expensive than they anticipated or can stretch to.

So their friend tells them *'Hey, Elance is cheap for that kind of stuff'* and so they desire – and build a brief for - that **same result** they already found (and have no room for influencing otherwise) for **one tenth of the cost.**

This is a perfect storm for bad apple clients, looking for an instruction taker, a laborer to deliver to precise instructions for the lowest possible cost in the quickest possible time.

It starts by understanding that online, deliberately increasing the size of your reach or 'footprint' into the areas dream clients ***begin their journey*** is a pivotal first move.

In this section we'll look at how your online footprint can be engineered so as to be visible *when and where* your clients begin to seek remedy for their pains.

Forbes, Inc. and the Kitchen Sink

"I wanted to work with creative entrepreneurs or writers, I can show up where they hang out, fairly easily so I made it an effort to become a blip on their radar" he said, so matter-of-factly that it was poetic.

We were barely two minutes into this Freelancelift Q&A call with designer and author Paul Jarvis and the value was already through the roof. I'd asked what the secret was to building exposure in a crowded space.

"I find that it's too daunting to go after everyone, so I focus it down into specific audiences. If your audience is 'the Internet' its more difficult, so if you can be the go-to-guy for a specialist audience it becomes a little easier to be seen"

- Paul Jarvis on Freelancelift Q&A

I couldn't agree more. As I covered earlier, our browsing habits become more sophisticated every day, we've learned to tune out anything that is potentially distracting. A strange benefit to this though, is that having access to so much information actually breeds a sense of loyalty when it comes to *where* we consume our information.

There are millions of blogs and resources out there, so we choose wisely and only keep a real eye on four or five, these – we feel – protect us from spam as their editorial and advertising filters are high.

Your dream client too chooses wisely, keeping an eye on their four or five trusted resources and consuming limited amounts of social media for wider context. When you look at it like that, in the context of your dream client's worldview does that make it easier? So where do they hang out?

In Paul's case, he made it a mission to be visible on sites like *Fast Company, Forbes, Inc., Lifehacker, Huffington Post* writing about issues his prospective audience **were already reading about.**

My first time around as a freelancer I saw arenas like these as *impenetrable fortresses*, where my dream clients bathed in anonymity and gorged on high-quality low salesmanship content inside, protected by their ability to block out everything else.

Top bracket freelancers like Paul take the **exact opposite stance** and see this as a strategic challenge - an objective they *must* achieve to extend their reach and increase the size of their online footprint. They strive to *be visible* in the areas their dream clients are *too loyal* to move away from.

- D Bnonn Tennant has a service that fit the bill for marketers and small businesses so he writes posts where 'Sam' hangs out, on **Unbounce.com or Kissmetrics.com**
- Nathan Barry sells books and courses to other designers, he posted stories to **Smashing Magazine and TutsPlus**
- Justin Jackson helps web developers and entrepreneurs so found a great amount of traction on **Hacker News and Reddit**

None of the three examples above find work on Elance, yet each one could fill the next three months of their schedules at the drop of a hat, for $100+ an hour.

You might think these guys are outliers, you may think you have some ground to build up to get anywhere near those guys. Both of these statements may well be true, but should that hold you back from starting? These are excuses, which encourage procrastination, its time stop them.

Plugging the gaps you're allowing to widen

Corbett Barr founded the awesome Fizzle.co video learning platform. I had asked what motivation and inspiration we could put to freelancers to **just get started**, to understand the importance of plugging the gaps between them and their peers.

Corbett echoed the benefits of building a platform:

"If you think about the sea of potential freelancers out there [to clients], it's really hard to compare one to the other, but if you find someone who has a platform talking about the issues you need solving you're going to pay attention."

- Corbett Barr on Freelancelift Q&A

Building a platform gives you the **competitive advantage** you need in an age where attention is diminished.

When going to market for a freelancer, prospective clients at the smarter end of the spectrum (the only ones we really want to do business with) will do their own research as to expertise level, your credibility and past work.

"It really comes down to making an investment in your business that isn't going to tangibly pay off right away. Just like offline networking, it might take a couple of months to have these relationships build into project work."

So what are you missing? If you're struggling to make an impact in your space then you probably have an issue in at least one of the following five areas.

The purpose of this book (and this evolution phase in particular) is to help you maximize all of these areas. Returning to the 'Theory of Constraints' philosophy we talked through earlier, it's important to **understand what is holding you back,** so that we can fix the broken parts and plug the gaps between our competitors and us.

1. You're not clear on who should know your name

In phase two we covered that you should be working hard to specialize **whom** your audience is. Who should care about you and your message? The objective of reducing your potential pool of customers is twofold; it makes it easier to identify and locate prospects and it *reduces the noise* of your competition.

With the 'difference statement' you developed earlier, you should have a clearer idea as to who should know your name. Being clear about this will make it much easier to keep an ear to the ground leave online breadcrumbs (more on that later) in locations you can be sure they'll be found.

2. You're not providing value

We've channeled the worldview of our dream client and by now hopefully you're in agreement that they do not particularly care about you (yet) and the skills you bring to the table unless what you are talking about positively effects them and their goals, or to be clearer; **what you're saying provides them with some value.**

Doesn't it appear strange that the lone religious preacher on a busy high street - who stands two feet taller than the crowd, has a megaphone in hand and a constant stream of words - gets *almost no attention?*

Online is no different, its much too easy for peers and prospects to simply walk on by if what you're saying holds no benefit to *them* and what they're trying to achieve.

If however the tact was not to bombard thousands of people with aimless diatribes, instead opting to spark up mutually beneficial conversations with a select few like-minded people, eventually leading to this same sermon, don't you think that would be more effective?

3. You're not visible outside of your own website

If you never reach out far enough to tell anyone your name, how will anybody know it? We've established that the over-arching purpose of attention is to improve your likelihood of acquiring new leads and sales for your freelance business.

It doesn't *start* there though. Unless you buy them for $5 you won't gather 1,000 Twitter followers overnight, you have to step outside the comfort of your current online footprint and introduce yourself to peers and prospective customers.

You also need to be prepared to tell your story. This gives you context and depth, even if it won't be consumed immediately. To overcome the 'I don't care' reflex you should tie your experiences to the struggle your dream clients (or indeed peers) are experiencing and a good story is useful for that purpose, building attention with empathy.

- What's your struggle?
- How did you overcome them
- Why do you do this?
- What are you most proud of?

Make moves to go and connect outside of your immediate circle. *Then* engage and **pull** visitors back to your site, the messaging you created in phase two will help you build brand recollection and justify this attention.

4. You provide no central 'hub' to engage with

Like the expert builder whose own roof is caving in, freelancers who operate in a creative / web space often neglect their own site, or go ultra-light on content opting for overly complex design ideas.

Or worse still, they don't have a site or blog at all - instead relying on a Dribbble or Behance portfolio to carry the strength of their brand.

So what do you think happens when someone likes what you have to say? How can they make that connection? How can they make their feelings felt?

Then what happens when your dream client tries to find you again on Dribbble only to be distracted by the featured work of a direct competitor?

This applies to non-creative service providers too, if you limit yourself to social media profiles as your central hub you leave the door open to distractions.

Even though you can like, favorite and otherwise engage with a piece of a portfolio or social profile does that platform really represent and define YOU? How does your same-same profile showcase you as anything *different?* You have nowhere to really make your messaging shine.

In particular I'm talking about ensuring you have a 'home' for your voice. A blog which transmits your message and your story in a shape of a short manifesto, your difference statement or another 'stake in the ground' outlining your intent.

You still can't prevent a visitor from leaving your site environment, but if you have in place something to capture and maintain that dialogue as well as a strong, clear and unique message you'll at least ensure you're not forgotten.

5. You're not looking to maintain dialogue

A crucial asset, which separates anonymous freelancers from those making real waves in their sector, is an ability to *maintain dialogue.*

The web is a very fickle place and often *gaining a new follower* just isn't enough. Specifically we're talking about exchanging a useful piece of content for an email address and maintaining dialogue with interesting and useful content thereafter.

In the next section we go into specifics, but suffice it to say if you can wrap your message into something of value to an audience the technology exists to easily package that as a PDF and add an opt-in mechanism to your site.

Widening your footprint

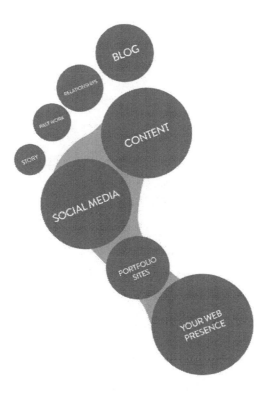

My job in this phase of the book is to show you that you're not exempt from marketing just because you're a freelancer. Sure, you're a one-person business and yes, you only need a handful of clients on a monthly basis to make this pay but this does not exempt you from *pushing your message*.

Like a business of any size you have operating costs, you have a requirement to make profit to survive and you have a product (service) to help you do that.

You can equate 'attention' to marketing, there is really no distinction between the two and this is the fundamental mindset shift that needs to happen before you're comfortable in going out and finding more of that attention. So what does the landscape look like for freelance businesses? Which elements make up your online footprint and how can they be engineered towards the worldview of your dream client? What follows is a breakdown of each of the areas shown.

Your web presence & blog

The importance of having a center point to your web presence is difficult to overstate. Put simply; it gives you the anchor point that is difficult to replicate with social profiles only.

In particular, your blog will be a fulcrum of your online voice and will support the additional activity you'll be undertaking to grow your online reputation and to ensure you are selected for the 'headline slot' over your peers.

A lot of this should be clear by now, but when it comes to influencing with value and engineering attention, a great web presence should:

Be an outlet for your voice

The amount of online attention you can command is hugely influenced by the exposure you can generate for your own messaging; generally via a great blog.

Introduce a valuable content piece

We'll talk about 'content' as an area shortly but your central web presence should lead a visitor to consuming content you're producing. Something infinitely valuable to your prospective audience enables you to retain dialogue and develop a longer-term relationship with a visiting dream client.

Be designed to attract conversion

Your site should enable and encourage otherwise passive visitors to convert into something of value to you. Specifically this means ensuring they have the smoothest path to conversion (whether that's sending you an email, completing a form or opting in to a content piece). You should be influence the answer to the following questions for each page, either with the words you use or the way a page is constructed:

- What should I **think** about this page?
- What should I **feel** about this page?
- What should I **do** on this page?

Every page on your site should have a logical next step; whether that's getting more information on a particular area of what you do or downloading a piece of takeaway content. Each page should have a purpose, to **advance the likelihood of conversion.**

Tell your story

We established the purpose and importance of laying out your messaging in phase two but it deserves underscoring here. Your reason for being should be *clearly represented*. Why are you different?

Visibility on portfolio sites which align with your skill

Portfolio sites can be a pain to keep up-to-date and sometimes they encourage spam, but sites like Dribbble don't have millions of users for no reason.

You should spread your message as far as you can beyond your own web presence in order that you're visible in every location your ideal persona potentially hangs out, so as to maximize that perception of relevant experience.

Make it a goal to add yourself to one new portfolio or community each month and try to make your presence felt, you'll be pleased with the result of this time investment.

A purposeful presence on social media

In social media (as in life) it's important that your presence is not too self-serving. Nobody likes *that guy* who only talks about himself a cocktail party, right? Social media is predicated on *sharing* but lots of users forget this.

You'll get more out of your social media presence by looking to it more objectively, as a:

- ✓ Networking tool
- ✓ Promotion tool
- ✓ Audience nurturing tool
- ✓ Customer service tool

When you aimlessly refresh your feed and achieve none of the above outcomes you're entering an area of procrastination and it's eating up your productivity.

When done well, each of these aspects combine to give you a solid foundation, which can eventually be converted into something of value to your business.

Social media is a fickle beast and to get the most out of it you should be utilizing it to serve all of those four areas, deliberately and equally.

Encourage sharing

There are several plugins and add-ons you have at your disposal for making each post and content piece you put together infinitely more shareable.

At the very least you should be using a plugin like 'Flare' which ads a simple floating share column to the right or left and side of your posts.

This is useful for the omnipresence and consistency that will support making content much easier to share.

Indeed, you can grab a suite of tools to help you make content shareable from SumoMe (by Appsumo) which will give you the ability to earmark paragraphs and statements to be shared directly from your posts as well as other more subtle tools to improve the volume of social shares on your posts and other content.

Automate your social media life

One of the most common reasons for a sporadic or inconsistent social media feed is simply a *lack of time* on the part of the freelancer to keep the channels up to date. If you aren't doing it already, you should understand the power of automation when it comes to social media.

Personally, I have the Buffer App on my iPhone, which allows me to pull in RSS feeds from the channels I pay attention to. It's then 20 minutes of curating and a few taps in a morning (literally from my bed) to schedule the updates for the next day or two.

You should definitely be reactive when it comes to social but its understandable that you won't be able to do it every day, so alternatively why not spend an hour or so per month to schedule tweets & Facebook updates into the future?

Hootsuite offers this straight out of the box and Buffer has now followed suit. Essentially you can upload a CSV containing one update per row. If you can create 60 updates en mass and have those be released over the period of a month you'll at least have a baseline of social updates to see you through when you're not able to work on social *that day.*

Understand the '3 Cs of social media'

Chances are you're doing social already, but have you ever asked why?

Do you have a clear objective for everything you do? Remember, we're trying to build attention and we do that by *providing value*. A few retweets here and there just won't cut it.

Your blog should give you starting point for the 'promotional' aspect of conversation and if you're providing value on that channel your updates will carry **depth and purpose.**

Then keep in mind the three C's when it comes to social, if your presence ticks all these boxes you have a recipe for a valuable, interesting set of profiles.

Creator
If you're looking to establish yourself as a thought leader, share great content and value **created by you.**

Curator
By curating great content from around the web that is of interest to your space you're establishing authority and above all great taste. If you're recognized as someone who is established in a particular topic it'll make it easier to justify why you would be a great as a service provider.

Chatterbox
Engaging in conversation on your feed isn't for everyone, but done well it establishes relationships which can then be taken outside of the social sphere. Likewise, adding your own insight and complimentary comments when sharing as a 'curator' is great for sparking conversations.

Successful social media accounts have a healthy mix of these three areas.

Providing value in your space with content

"Either write something worth reading, or do something worth writing about."
Benjamin Franklin

In his post "Words – This is a webpage" (which to date has had over 200,000 page views) Justin Jackson lays out a beautifully simple example of the *power of words*.

We can sometimes get too wrapped up in the presentation, messaging, design and promotion of content that we forget about the content itself.

"I wrote this in a text editor. It's 6KB. I didn't need a Content Management System, a graphic designer, or a software developer. There's not much code on this page at all, just simple markup for paragraphs, hierarchy, and emphasis."

The basis for all communication is words. Whether those are written, heard or seen the same is true for all languages. So if your job is to communicatively engage and build attention then it pays to understand the power of content as a medium.

Define; content

Content - in this context at least - can best be described as relevant information *aligned with or explaining your product or service.* When used for commercial ends, content should have a clear audience, drive demand and make starting a relationship with an otherwise passive visitor easier (note I said easier, not easy!).

Composing content such as blog posts, ebooks, videos, audio and more can help you drive traffic, generate leads and nurture – by educating - your prospective clients.

Your content should educate, inspire and teach. Here are five characteristics you should always consider when looking to inspire positive sentiment with your content.

1. Don't "always be closing"

Unless you're dealing with an exceptional circumstance try not to be overly promotional it'll leave your recipients or readers feeling a little cold. Nobody likes to feel suckered into a covert sales pitch. Try to inspire, excite and provide room for thought on the part of your dream client.

2. Keep it original & close to the messaging you've defined

If you put out generic content that could just as easily be found on about.com or other content farms you will find it difficult to inspire engagement. It should be useful, actionable and support the core message we defined in phase two. Generic, irrelevant content (from the worldview of your prospective client) will trigger the 'ignore' reflex you're fighting against in your quest for attention.

3. Teach, but build intrigue and demand

By developing content that gives "tip of the iceberg" messaging and addresses a pain or a problem your prospect is facing you'll create a sense of curiosity that pushes a dream client closer to your "buy" zone.

Without resorting to deception, try to leave some ideas open or push users in the direction of other content, to engineer a hunger for understanding more.

4. It has to be constructed well

I say "constructed" here rather than "written" as we're including all content types within that broad term so if you're putting out videos make sure you are audible and the lighting is good, if you're producing a book make sure the file layout is legible and if you're writing a blog post, it has to be grammatically beautiful.

5. Show an element of proof

How have you cured this pain for others? You can use real-life case studies, wrap it in your messaging to build demand and intrigue, you should be looking to inspire the *aha moment "maybe they can do this for me"*.

If you frame it within the worldview of your dream you'll build a bond of trust that'll make the prospect infinitely easier to sell to when the time comes.

Emulate Hansel & Gretel

We're all familiar with the 1812 fable Hansel & Gretel, but there is a business analogy nestling between the lines most will not be familiar with.

You'll recall that Hansel scattered breadcrumbs to find a path home for him and his sister to safeguard against a potentially ill-fated journey.

As a freelancer - like the siblings in this story - you are one of a *whole forest* of service providers vying for attention.

You have a space in a dark corner of the web, so if you have no 'breadcrumbs', signals or signposts leading potential dream clients to your door you're always going to struggle with a lack of attention.

Every time you make an insightful blog comment, each time you strike up a relationship on social media, every time you publish a video, portfolio piece or forum comment you're **leaving a breadcrumb**.

Over time, the more breadcrumbs you scatter around the web leading back to you and your message the louder your voice becomes and the more hungry peers and prospects you have beating a way to your door.

When was the last time you made a concerted effort to leave a *piece of yourself* somewhere other than on your own platforms? All of these breadcrumbs have a purpose to lead a prospective client into a territory where *you* control the message. If you can put in the work to leverage a trail of breadcrumbs in this way it can be highly lucrative for you and your freelance business.

Breadcrumbs or 'satellites' can include videos on YouTube and Vimeo, images on Instagram and Pinterest, social media updates on Twitter, Facebook, LinkedIn and Google Plus. They could also take the shape of infographics, guest posts, blog comments, ebooks, display advertising, email newsletters and the list goes on.

These morsels of content, if situated correctly, will drive the right kind of attention to your door.

Commit to producing valuable content consistently

I talked to Nathan Barry recently, who built the app 'Commit' which aims to help you build healthy habits. In Nathan's case, he committed to writing 1,000 words a day and did so for 600+ days before changing his goal.

If you can make a small time investment like this, once a day and produce valuable content consistently you'll have the foundations in place to multiply exposure and build your platform.

Are you posting in forums? Do you provide a ton of email support? What about general dialogue with peers you're offering advice to? Do you generally give advice to others via social media? Do you have some killer explanatory text in your proposal templates?

This is all 'content' and you'd be surprised how much of it you plough through without realizing. The smart freelancer understands that this has value beyond its original purpose and uses these techniques to produce valuable content consistently.

When I talked to Amy Hoy, a former freelance developer and founder of a $1m software company we discussed that her first PDF book was a culmination of the blog posts and forum comments she'd put together on the topic of Ruby-on-Rails.

She collated these into a structured resource, an ebook which she still sells copies of today and which has generated over $90k in revenue in that time.

Content is all around you, commit to building it at least on a bi-weekly basis and make it count.

Hit it big with epic content

Are there content pieces (blog posts, videos, guides) that you continually circle back to when you need clarity on a certain topics? If you have a problem with productivity, marketing or social media maybe you probably look up a certain post that sticks in your mind.

You'll often hear these being recommended as *'essential reading for fundamental understanding'* on a particular issue or topic area.

These comprehensive run-downs can best be described as 'pillar content' pieces as the content generally achieves 'pillar' status in its field for a period of years. To be more precise, they are renowned due to their depth and density. They are 'epic'.

So what is 'epic content'?

Epic doesn't have to mean long, it doesn't have to mean perfectly designed or written... it should just mean *highly valuable.*

If you're ready to hit publish on a post, and you can answer this question positively you probably have something epic:

'Does this have the power to change someone's course in life and business when they find this in a few months or years? Will it stick in their head so much that they'll return to it and refer it to others long after the date of publish?'

Not every content piece needs to be epic though, if you had 3-4 pillar posts from 50 on your blog you'd have a significant amount of momentum and in turn the exposure you need to turn this momentum into attention, and ultimately something of value to your business.

Try Video

Video isn't for everyone, but now that most of world's population thinks nothing of carrying around a *high definition* camera capable of super-slow motion in their pocket (iPhone) there are fewer and fewer excuses for not putting out video.

You are solving problems on a daily basis for you, your clients, and your peers so if you can wrap those into value-driven videos you'll have a great head start on the 80% in your space that won't bother.

Kickstarting content production

If you still have that nagging, irrational phobia towards writing or producing content here are some ideas to getting started quickly. As you begin to be more confident you'll find the need for these 'prompts' will lessen.

Recycle stuff you've already said

Old email threads in which you've explained points or Q&A responses can all be classed as content and built upon to produce blog posts or downloadable content. If you can get to the essence of what you were trying to say at the time and you can build a post around it you'll have ammunition for a steady flow of content.

Just talk

If writing doesn't come naturally, maybe talking does. If you record yourself talking with authority on any subject you're just a transcription away from a blog post outline.

The best advice I have is to mindmap everything you'd like to talk about so it flows and has structure. Record this into your smartphone or even the microphone on your computer and dispatch that off to be transcribed.

My transcriber of choice is magiscript.com – Lainie and her teamwork wonders, removing the umms, aahs, and spaces along with structuring the content with headers, sub-heads and more.

If you can chat for just 4 or 5 minutes you'll have a 600+ word blog post that just requires some small amendments and publishing. Try it.

Ghostwriter

Provided you're not writing a piece on intricate brain surgery you should be able to team up with an experienced writer who can put posts together matching your general style.

Expect to pay around $0.05-15 per word for ghost writing. I recommend Tom Ewer or Content Hero.

Delivering value-by-email

If you have systems in place to maintain dialogue with your audience and you're providing value-by-email you can *teach your way* to better brand recognition. You should consider every email communication you put out to subscribers as marketing.

When compared to general social media and outbound activity email is incredibly effective. If you have 1,000 followers, only 5-10% of those may actually see your tweet (before it gets buried beneath updates from other users they follow), that's an opportunity for maybe 50 or 100 people to see it, for an hour maximum at that.

Yet if you email 1,000 engaged opt-ins, you can achieve open rates of 40% and beyond. What's more, the email will be visible in their inbox indefinitely.

In terms of ensuring ongoing attention, you should take email (and the gathering of email addresses in the first place) very seriously. Here are some ideas.

Nurture an email list by giving your knowledge away

It's becoming infinitely easier to 'teach your way to the sale', even as a freelancer. In this way, we're using the concept of *inbound marketing*.

'Inbound' can best be described as *permission based* marketing, so you have made connection – being given a prospect's email on your site - but you realize there is a whole series of other objections you must overcome in the mind of your client, so you use this implied permission to send content and insight which overcomes these objections and lays out why you might be a good fit.

You should be able to answer comfortably:

- Can I trust this person to do this work for me?
- Are they skilled enough to produce me something excellent?

- Have they done it before?
- What will this mean to my business and me?

If you look to *nurture* your list once you've captured their email, with content that goes some way to assuring you have a clear answer to those objections you'll be in a very strong position to command the attention that'll see you at the front of the herd, rather than in the middle somewhere.

You can 'teach' with screencasts, blog posts, videos, ebooks, hangouts on Google+ whatever it takes to ease your audience into you and your message.

Create a follow-up email sequence

In order to nurture your prospects with content via email you're going to need to set up a follow-up (also known as an 'autoresponder') sequence of emails.

These will be received by the prospect over a fixed period of time. You can set these up relatively inexpensively using Campaign Monitor, MailChimp or a great platform GetDrip.com (3 months free with this link).

In any of those cases you're normally starting the relationship with some interesting introductory content ('Hey, download this thing of value' not 'OI, sign up for my newsletter') and then continuing this relationship via email with a follow-up sequence.

Syndicate your content

Sites like Quora and Medium offer a great way to broadcast your message further than your current online circle allows. Utilizing both, you can have a blog set up in 10 minutes, which you can then re-post your own blog content to.

If you're active in the Quora community too you'll build up 'credits', which you can use to *boost posts* so that they appear right in front of your prospective audience.

This is a great way to ensure you get maximal exposure for every post you create and it a way to reach out to a wider audience without incurring monetary cost.

In some way we're at a crossroads when it comes to content. If you'd asked me 4 years ago what the point of producing content was the word 'SEO' would have probably reared its head. With that would quickly follow 'but it has to be unique'.

Times change.

Nowadays you can syndicate (yep, duplicate) your content to credible external platforms, benefit from a bigger online footprint and drive traffic from the masses of users on those platforms.

Something (five figures to be exact) out of nothing

"Charlie will be with you shortly", chirped the affable receptionist. Leaning over the huge glass desk, she politely gestured that I make myself comfortable. I headed towards the oversized, fashionable furniture at the side of the foyer area and took a seat.

A rye smile broke across my face as I realized the gravity of what I was about to do. *Charlie* was Head of Digital at Universal Music Europe (yes, *that* Universal) and I had just travelled by train from Manchester to their beautifully appointed London headquarters to meet about three new web projects.

My second time around as a freelancer I realized the power of specificity. I had figured out that in order to *maximize* my chances of working with dream clients I had to *minimize* the potential pool of customers.

Given my exposure to the music industry, and my penchant for design 'web designer for the bands, artists and independent record labels' was difference statement I chose and I'm glad I did.

Just four months earlier I was still working in my corporate position, balancing a freelancing sideline with my day-to-day activities. During those final few months I was able to build a new business in the same way I've advised in this book; a brand with a unique outlook, positioned correctly and committed to evolution.

This brand still stands today, as does the site (brandshank.com). This was my outlook in early 2011, what was next?

- ✓ I had committed to evolution and mapped out my goals, this really helped me focus on what I needed to achieve and how
  Phase one, check

- ✓ I had mapped out my specialized, dream client profile and built solid touchpoints, which carried unique messaging
  Phase two, check

✓   That was all well and good, but nobody knew who I was?
Enter, phase three

I implemented everything we've spoken about already in this phase, committing to providing value with great content *(this post alone generated over 600 social media shares, 71 comments and 14 solid business enquiries)* and had made a concerted effort to leverage my exposure within the industry to do social media well.

The client enquiries began to come which was great, but I had a problem. They didn't quite match the blueprint I had for my ideal client in one crucial area: budget.

I had the foundations in place and I could have just stopped there, continued in that fashion with revenue of maybe $5,000 per month indefinitely.

But I knew my dream client was out there, who could help me achieve my objective of $10,000 per month in revenue, *I just needed connections* to bigger and better places, I needed a portfolio of work that impressed the higher bracket clients I was looking for and I needed **relationships.**

In the months that followed I was able to make connections with bands and artists *whom I had never contacted* before they received that first email from me.

I've laid out my insight in this area on the following pages, but to close the loop on this part of the story I was able to secure two pieces of work, both internationally renowned artists.

I was working for free but had full creative control and these projects became mine to showcase, an example of top-level prior work with happy testimonials to show for it.

They were happy, they had a great end-result for no cost. I was happy; I had two dream client examples, which gave me a huge amount of leverage. Who would ever know (or care) what I was paid for it?

Then came a moment of magic, the introductory email from Seb (the manager of one of the artists I'd done free work for).

"Hi Liam, it's Seb, hope you're well. I'd like to introduce you to Charlie, he's Head of Digital at Universal who liked the work you did for [artist] and has some projects he'd like to talk to you about."

So off to London I was!

In the two years that followed, the relationship with Universal delivered projects with a combined revenue of mid five figures *(Universal redacted the real number, spoilsports)* and worked with Seb for several further projects, all paid for fully.

Here's what I took away and how I advise you to look at building relationships, remember to **equate attention with marketing**. That is to say, anything you're doing to build relationships (which you will inevitably 'spend' time on, including free work) is no different to the retailer who 'spends' money on a pre-Christmas TV ad slot.

Each has the same outcome, attention. Use free work sparingly, as I've detailed on the following pages then supplement it with other relationship building activity outlined.

Leveraging cold email

As a designer for the music industry, the obvious goal before I started out was to work with dream clients such as Universal and Virgin Records. Winning these types of customer isn't easy though. You need a track record.

So, I began to map out a route. In any industry there is a pyramid of excellence. If your dream client is at the very top then *they need to be sure* you've performed at a level sufficient to theirs.

By strategically working for free - only with clients you feel can help raise your own profile - you can build up your portfolio and gain this track record, a shortcut up the pyramid if you will.

Although you won't be getting paid for the work per se, those few days you spend delivering a top-notch service to those clients could mean a position in the driving seat for dream client *paying customers* in the future.

So where do you start?

Your Hitlist

We've already outlined who our dream client is, so you should look to profile who these are and what their characteristics are.

Don't be afraid to look for the level *below* the top if necessary. I recommend building clear criteria for your 'stepping stone' client. Take this as an example:

- Client must have credibility in their area of expertise.
- The brand must be recognizable and established.
- The brand must be connected and relevant to my vision.

Creating a specific list of 'stepping stone' clients is rather simple – you should have a go right now. Once you have established who your ideal client is, you can begin to draw a personal path to the top of the pyramid.

Get started

You should get to know the parties you want to reach out to first, understand the issues they're facing and the things they have in the pipeline that you could help with. You can often get nuggets of this information by reading between the lines of blog posts and social media updates.

If you know that a brand is launching a new offshoot, offer to assist with some consultancy as to the UI flow (designer), copy (writer) or infrastructure migration (coder) for example. Or if their current site or product could be better, point out **how** and indicate that you believe in their direction and would be prepared to lend a hand on a voluntary basis.

It only takes two or three good case studies with great clients to ensure your previous work stands out from the crowd. By specializing in on an audience too, logos and brands you've worked with become more relevant and you naturally 'borrow' some of the credibility from those brands.

Forget for a second that you're working for free here but don't let your other client obligations slip, consider this a promotional activity.

Speed of execution is not the deciding factor here, a solid, well thought out approach is. Quality matters, so keep your current clients happy while going down this route.

The backwards sales pitch

Here is where it gets interesting, you want to present what you've completed in such a way that it appears a no-brainer for your prospect to use in some way.

You're providing the solution first, working backwards from there to **agree a fee of zero.**

You should approach your prospect in a mature, sensitive way that matches their personal preferences. This normally manifests itself as email but more recently Social media can work, as can being visible within groups and in the comments are for posts being pushed by the 'stepping stone' client.

With that said here's a *backwards sales pitch* email you can swipe right now :

Subject:
An idea/feedback for [prospect-name] [your-skill] enhancement/improvement

Dissected: There is no mention of an offer here; you're providing *ideas* or feedback for enhancement first. This starts the dialogue in a collaborative tone.

The subject is the most important element here, but within the body content you should address:

-   A particular pain point this prospect might have (Tip: A globally true pain or fear is being overtaken by competitors)
-   That this is in no way a pitch, only a contribution from a follower with ideas
-   That a reply is optional, you'd be just pleased they consumed it. This is known as 'an easy out'. Arguing against the primary purpose of your contact is a surefire way to ensure you *do* get a response.

Here's a quick example:

Hey Liam,

Love what you're doing on Freelancelift, just wanted to touch base and give you some feedback on a point you raised in a recent post by you on evolution as a freelancer and in particular having processes in place.

I have tons of experience in project management [content writing for conversion, plugin development etc.] and just put some thought into a quick process template [big content idea, development improvement idea] which I thought I'd share.

This approach has no ulterior motive just wanted to return the favor of you providing your expertise to me, by at least giving you something that I've learned from my 5 years' experience in design.

I also note that you're in a bit of a head-to-head battle with YourCompetitor.com and this is something they're just not doing either.

Anyway, appreciate your time in getting this far, I've compiled the ideas here:

::Link::

If I don't hear back from you that's cool, appreciate you're busy. For now I've kept this work between me and you and you have my permission to use it, with no cost. But just let me know if you've done that so I can jump for joy on my social channels.

Alternatively I can chat through with you how this might pan out if you wanted me to develop on this idea a little further.

My Skype is XYZ or hit reply,
Sign-off

Invest in relationships

Understand that one piece of free ('marketing') work that takes you a few days to complete could result in wider attention via social media or in some of the blogs and trusted platforms your dream client hangs out in, not to mention the opportunities for word of mouth referrals (like with the Seb & Charlie example).

Neil Patel is the co-founder at Kissmetrics and CrazyEgg and operates a kick-ass blog at Quicksprout.com, during his recent Freelancelift Q&A call he underlined the value of relationships.

"You need to go out there and talk about good stuff, then invest in those relationships by reaching out to the bloggers and potential clients in your space"

- Neil Patel on Freelancelift Q&A

Here are some actionable tips for building relationships outside of cold email.

Be visible on the blogs and communities in your space

Popular blogs in your industry, frequented by your peers (not dream clients in this instance) can be a great place to build relationships. By striking up conversations and being visible in your space you multiply your chances of being cited as a resource or being introduced to potential dream clients.

The benefits of connecting with industry influencers are numerous but include:

- Social shares of your content to a larger audience
- Guest post opportunities
- Referral opportunities
- Interview opportunities, them citing you as a resource in your specialism
- Direct quotes for your own content (to add weight)

In particular, if your audience is highly specialized and an influencer is asked by a member of their audience for help finding someone with your skillset they will always recommend the person that is contributing the most to their community.

If you're looking to start an online relationship with an *influential peer* in your sphere it's better to have been a 'blip on their radar' before you make the first move and connect.

An easy way to do this is to be active on their web presence in a way that is open and non-intrusive, such as leaving comments or sharing content.

The second potential benefit of being an active contributor to discussions is the visibility and authority you might generate with parties who may eventually be your clients.

Blogs and online brands with a good amount of comments (average 10-30) per post are perfect, as these will have an active, engaged audience.

Too many and you'll be lost in the mire, too few and you'll find it to be a bit of a ghost town. Make yourself known for adding examples, breaking down ideas and providing your own spin and you'll be surprised at how much trust this will build with all parties.

Approaching influencers directly

Making insightful comment is just one of the ways you can connect with influencers. This generally is the first step towards something more meaningful.

But guess what? Everyone is trying to do the same thing, any 'voice' in your space with a relevant, engaged audience probably receives upwards of 50 cold emails a day so it does take a little care and a lot of patience to get right.

Just as in the offline world, great relationships are not created out of one, cold approach they are built and nurtured over time.

Here is my take on approaching influencers:

1. Build a target list of around 20 influencers whose message, outlook and audience match your own
2. You must be confident they (and their audience) would get value from your content and have something you'd like their opinion on
3. Have an engagement map (to ensure you're visible on their radar)
   a. Two blog comments
   b. Follow on Twitter
   c. Two tweets
   d. Two shares of their posts on social
4. Personally email to make a more real connection with a purpose

This 'purpose' could simply be a second look at one of your own content pieces it could be to introduce yourself and ask for an interview which you can house on your own site but the idea is to send that email with a distinct goal in mind in order that you can be sure of a response.

Answer questions on Q&A sites

You have a great opportunity to establish expertise and an authority level in your space by utilizing Q&A platforms. In the online space you have a few options:

- Quora
- Clarity
- Reddit
- Stackoverflow (Tech & programming)

The idea here is to be **visible as an authority** in your area and surprisingly few freelancers follow this technique through. There are lots of questions your ideal client persona will be posing, as will your peers.

As all of your responses will provide reference (a 'breadcrumb') back to your central web presence they will prove infinitely valuable in the long run.

Seek out partners in a parallel market

Do you write content? Team up with a web designer. If you're a coder, team up with a marketer. The point here is to surround yourself with potential partners who have:

a) Virtually the same audience
b) Services that don't directly compete with yours

As a freelancer, you're probably used to having your clients ask you the question (in the example of a web designer) "can you do branding? or "Do you know anyone who could help with the copy for the site?"

If you had a semi-formal agreement with several other freelancers to give you a trusted outlet for these types of queries you'd have the double benefit of pleasing your client as well as helping out your partner, this could be commission based or just be backed by 'goodwill'

When this is reciprocated it's a great feeling, so have a think how you can team up with partners in a parallel market for mutual gain.

Private communities & mastermind groups

In my opinion, generic 'forums' are a preserve of 20th Century online activity. It has been superseded by more mature, multi-channel communication methods, which incorporate social channels.

There are several great 'closed doors' communities though where freelancers and solopreneurs speak openly about what is working for them.

I would recommend joining at least one community; the relationships you build here along with the accountability element will have great knock-on benefits for your online voice.

- Fizzle ($35/m Fizzle membership)
  - o Includes Fizzle library video training
- Workshop Community ($64/m)
  - o Includes daily freelance leads-by-email
- Freelancelift Pro ($65/m)
  - o Includes video library and monthly coaching calls

Offline

When was the last time you went to an event in your space? As online service providers we tend to forget there is a 'real world' out there. Even if you are in a relatively tight vertical there will still be an event, talk, meet up that's right for you.

When it comes to cementing relationships online, there are very few scenarios that do a better job than meeting in person, in an informal setting (especially if alcohol is involved) so see what events are in your space and do what you can to build relationships that help enhance your online footprint.

Implement traditional advertising

As a business, you have a virtually unlimited amount of options available to you for traditional online advertising methods.

With Twitter ads you can figure out which accounts they follow, and target ads only to that audience. With Facebook you can target by interest, demographic and the fan pages they're likely to be subscribed to.

It's not uncommon to achieve a visitor cost of $0.40. If you had 100 targeted visitors matching the profile of a dream client landing on a great piece of content you've put together do you think you'll be able to generate more than $40 in revenue from those visits over time?

Once you've established a solid reputation you should seek to supplement natural traffic with paid activity, even if you're just carrying out a 'toe in the water' exercise.

You could be visible with Google Adwords for the phrases your target audience might be searching for, or you could have a banner ad appear on their favorite blog going through a platform such as BuySellAds.

Don't limit yourself *just* to content, or *just* to relationship building. Multiply the potential outlets for your message and increase your exposure to reach a reputation level your dream clients will find it difficult to ignore.

Download full versions of the tools, resources and worksheets which support this book, by heading to freelancelift.com/book

Do one thing every day that grows your footprint

"Do one thing every day that scares you."
Eleanor Roosevelt / Baz Lurhmann

If you take steps daily to build your online voice not only though do you build an authority, an online presence and a platform, you begin to widen your net of relationships with your peers, influencers and dream clients in your space.

Growing in online stature can – and indeed should – be done incrementally. The inspiration for this request of you for a 'mini commitment' comes from the Baz Lurhmann track – *Wear Sunscreen* which recites the essay 'Advice, like youth, probably just wasted on the young' by *Mary Schmich*.

If you ask yourself every day "what did I do today to grow my online exposure" you have the perspective required to take decisive action. Below is a checklist you can take and refer back to daily, to give you inspiration for completing small goals, regularly.

Dependent on the amount you invest in this, and the number of ideas you put into practice from this phase of evolution, you'll start to see the fruits of your labor in a matter of weeks or months.

It's difficult, I get it. A client with a tight deadline or a project that just *needs to be finished* will almost always come ahead of finishing 'that blog post' or updating 'that profile'.

My hope is that buying into a small commitment, **doing just one thing**, **every day** that grows your online footprint will make it feel manageable, and will enable you to multiply your exposure and build your platform.

I ♥
freelancelift

- ❑ Had a tweet of mine retweeted
- ❑ Published a guest post on another site
- ❑ Uploaded a video to Youtube
- ❑ Engaged in a Q&A on a site like Quora
- ❑ Spoke to a reputable voice on Clarity
- ❑ Made a helpful comment on a blog post
- ❑ Interviewed an "A list" voice to be used on my site
- ❑ Retweeted a post of someones and was thanked
- ❑ Submitted a useful answer in a forum in my space
- ❑ Got access to Dribbble (or other invite-only network)
- ❑ Had an email exchange with a reputable voices
- ❑ Provided some useful advice in a parallel market
- ❑ Agreed to have a reputable voice post on my blog
- ❑ Had a personal thank you email from one of my email sends
- ❑ Attended an offline event in my space (helps online!)
- ❑ Published a podcast to iTunes
- ❑ Had a comment on my own blog
- ❑ Got access into a closed mastermind group
- ❑ Published a blog post

Aim for 1-3 from this list per day

Download full versions of the tools, resources and worksheets which support this book, by heading to freelancelift.com/book

Phase IV

Level out the income rollercoaster, build predictability into the model

Nestled on the North West shore of England is Blackpool, an often conflicted theme park town a mere 46 miles from my front door.

In July 2007, Blackpool played host to Richard Rodriguez, a veteran dare devil who embarked on a feat that would land him a place in the Guinness book of records.

The challenge was to successfully complete the *world's longest roller coaster marathon* and the crowds descended. He had a marker of nine days and two hours to beat.

At around the same time I was riding a roller coaster of my own, 22 years old and battling hard to keep afloat as a self-employed service provider.

As freelancers we work with - and *just accept* - a paradigm of unpredictability. Instead of putting in place mechanisms that might help us beat it, we *'do a Richard'* and just keep on riding that 'coaster.

It took the sour taste of failure to help me realize that as a freelancer it doesn't *have* to be this way. Sure, there is unpredictability and the same is true for all small businesses but there are **three distinct ways** to build predictability into the model.

This information is the piece of the jigsaw that was missing for me last time around, so in this phase of evolution I want to lay out what these stabilizing factors are in order that you can put them to work in your own business.

Permitted only five minutes break for every full hour of riding, the pace was relentless for Richard. A constant barrage of wind and rain swept in from the

Irish Sea, which added to the already unhealthy doses of G-force and torturous monotony.

Sounds like the bad weeks as a freelancer, right?

Richard managed to break the world record - much to the delight of the infinitely polite British onlookers - almost doubling the previous effort, riding *The Big One* and *Big Dipper* for a total of 405 hours and 40 minutes, almost 17 days straight.

We aren't here to break records and you can be sure we're in it for significantly longer than 17 days, but what can we put in place to break from the metaphoric roller coaster experience and what do we mean when we say 'stable'?

Quantifying stability

For me, stability can be quantified as a *dependable revenue of around 25-50% your average monthly income.*

So for example, if on average you earn $5,000 per month as a freelancer you'll feel a lot more stable in your position if you knew you could rely on $1,250-2,500 every month being taken care of without having to go and find ncw freelance clients.

This is the sweet spot, the point at which you can commit to *that vacation* or the other life decisions requiring a little forward planning financially. Stability of income is the Achilles heel of freelancing, the potential death knell that never really goes away.

In this phase of the book we'll tackle it. I want you to keep the financial elephant in the room at least well fed if we can never really evict it entirely. In doing so you'll feel happier generally and look forward to applying your craft rather than applying for that credit card.

It starts by understanding there are really only *three ways* to do this.

1. Be the indispensible asset

If you position yourself as a mutually beneficial partner to a client, you can develop the trust and goodwill that will deliver regular, dependable business from a pool of repeat clients.

In the pages that follow, we'll investigate how this starts and what you need to have in place to facilitate these longer-term, win-win partnerships.

2. Productize your expertise to supplement your earnings

Creating a product - a profitable side project - which isn't tied to you or your hourly rate is a key weapon in the fight against instability. You are solving problems for clients (and indeed peers) on a daily basis, so you have the baseline ingredients and expertise to build a product. This can stand-alone and develop a revenue stream to offset the unstable weeks.

3. Enable more pricing choice and recurring billing options

When it comes to pricing tiers and 'bolt-on' options, less is certainly not more. When faced with options in a transactional scenario, we have natural tendencies to gravitate towards particular options. If you can leverage this pricing psychology and give your clients the opportunity to continue paying you long after the project is complete you can tap into another indispensible supplementary income stream.

Be the partner and indispensible asset

It was the third time in a row I'd run the numbers. Something had to be wrong.

Maybe it was a quirk between Excel and Mac, demons of conflicting technologies conspiring against me, or maybe some of the numbers going into the spreadsheet were flawed but no, each time I calculated it the same conclusion was met.

It's October 2014 and we've had a great few years, I had a hunch that we (*Tone - the web agency that sprouted from my fledgling freelance business*) did pretty well from repeat clients and I wanted to pull together the actual data.

It was a staggering statistic.

Of the 212 previous customers 58% had come back to spend again within 12 months of their initial order, a rarity in web design and an achievement in itself. Then of the clients that did return, each spent an average 136% of their initial order over an 18-month period.

Simplistically, this meant that for every $10 spent today, an additional $8.10 would be spent over the next 18 months, from the same pool of clients.

It was difficult to relate this to anything tangible at first, but then I found the number that baffled me into thinking it was wrong.

The trend suggested that it would be entirely possible within 6-12 months for the business to have *enough repeat customers* at the correct spend levels to not need to find **any** new clients at all!

To demonstrate the magnitude of this in a freelancer perspective, let's say you earned an average of $5,000 per month in 2014 – your annual revenue at that point is $60,000.

So what if, over the following 18 months you could be *statistically sure* that you'd realize a further $48,000 from that same bunch of clients?

That's a cool $2,650 **every month** from clients you know and with whom you enjoy working for the next year and a half.

What would that do the stability of your business?   Would that help take away the 'up then down' roller coaster feelings?

$2,650 a month probably covers your overheads, it ensures you can live a little, cover your mortgage and keep food on the table. You have a baseline of clients who will ensure you don't go hungry and you have a little more creative freedom to say 'NO' when a potential bad apple shows up.

The power of partnership

The power of partnership is something I'm only really realizing now, after having these principles in place for a long enough period of time and I'd like to show you how to do the same.

For some of our clients we are not 'just web designers', nor are we nameless suppliers, we are **indispensable business assets.** We've built enough trust and a strong enough relationship with some clients to ensure there are no other options; hence they come back again and again.

I'd certainly not planned for this, I cannot claim this as a masterstroke on my part but it soon became apparent how it came to pass. We've instilled a *spirit of partnership* within the team at Tone when it comes to dealing with every new client. An aspiration for *World Class* output and communication, which permeates every touch point.

This brings us stability as a business now and a baseline of revenue we feel we can rely on.   It started for me when I understood the difference between a partner (that indispensible asset to a client) and a laborer (the *useful but throwaway* instruction taker). Which do you aspire to be?

Laborer vs. Partner

There are shades of grey between these two polar opposites, but empirically there are only two types of freelancer, the *partner* and the *laborer.*

The Laborer

You may have utilized the services of a laborer in the past, perhaps for the heavy lifting of data entry, some coding you just couldn't stretch to or maybe they helped you with some content entry once.

There is definitely a place for a laborer; it's just not a place I'd like you to operate in. You will find laborers aplenty on Fiverr. Working to *very specific* outcomes with a precise, *low cost* and swift delivery.

You'll also find them among a sea of web professionals on Elance and perhaps in your junk folder purporting to provide SEO or link building.

The Partner

Partners take the time to understand clients deeply, investing themselves in the client message and establishing an expertise that isn't easily pigeonholed.

That is to say, as a partner you'll put yourself forward as a person to be trusted, to have as a sounding board and a thoroughfare to other experts. A partner ends up being an indispensible asset to any business, building a mutually beneficial relationship.

The grey area

At this point, I'm hoping you have elected yourself out of the laborer group but there is a grey area, that you may fall into inadvertently and which you should know about. Here's the thing, bad apple clients have the *ability to make laborers out of partners.*

Earlier in the book I talked about well researched - in their mind at least - clients arriving at your door with pre-conceived ideas of what they need and a sturdy - again, in their mind - brief.

I covered that at this point it's too late to influence their outlook, so you should be vigilant to spot these characteristics before they arise.

You know the type; midway through the project you wished you'd never even agreed to take the project. In the end you accept any request without question in the hope that there may be light at the end of the tunnel and that it'll soon all be over.

Unfortunately, at that point you've been ground down to a laborer status, even if you started off with the best intentions.

How communication facilitates partnership

A partner has a much higher likelihood of long-term, stable income from their clients and you should look to break away from the 'project mindset', the thinking that a client is here today, gone tomorrow and eventually replaced.

A veteran of freelancing, with an impressive 26 years experience is Shawn Hesketh. Now founder at wp101.com and with a quarter century under his belt as a freelancer I was delighted to speak to him on a Freelancelift Q&A call.

On the call, Shawn dug into his own unique take, recommending an approach centered on taking the time to deeply understand a client's business. What their market is, who their competitors are, their problems and they way they handle themselves.

"I realized what I most enjoyed was really connecting with a client, you're investing a tremendous amount of time to create the best possible product so why not leverage that insight to make suggestions which may entail using your services again."

For Shawn this resulted in a healthy line of partner-focused relationships lasting an average 4-6 years per client.

"Ensuring everyone is on the same page is critical to a successful partnership. Effective communication begins with careful listening with intent. How well are you communicating with your clients?"

-       Shawn Hesketh on Freelancelift Q&A

Account for over delivery but clearly state when you do it

As a species we become accustomed to new experiences very quickly. You only have to go on vacation for longer than a couple of weeks to almost settle in as if it were your home.

If you consistently over deliver your clients will see this as the **new normal.** In most cases this isn't a problem, but what about that time you deliver *'as expected'*? You're now underperforming against this 'new normal' precedent.

I advocate expecting a 10-20% over delivery and building this into your price (without explicitly showing it in your costs of course). A good client will not quibble pre-project over a fee for the sake of 10%, yet the trust built from not billing extra at every juncture mid-project will go a long way.

This is especially true when you explicitly tell the client you're over delivering. Here's an example line you can use:

"I just wanted to let you know that while the scope of the project didn't actually include [over delivered item] I would like to do it for you, in the spirit of partnership at no additional cost."

Over delivery and excellent service are to be encouraged and applauded, but you need to make it clear that this is *not* normal practice. You can check out my short book 'Nice Freelancers Finish Last' which echoes a similar kind of sentiment.

Manage expectations to shape long-term trust

Do clients care if the project runs 3 days over the deadline? If you tell them the night before the proposed completion date then sure, expect the wrath!

If you communicate it to them 3 weeks ahead and back it up with valid reasoning and a message which echoes this spirit of partnership the outcome will be very different. So why the differing response to what is, effectively the same net result?

Put simply, communication.

It seems so obvious yet it's the most common reason larger - potentially dream client - businesses will opt for using an agency instead of a better-qualified freelancer.

Dream clients look out for - and expect - solid communication, consistency and long-term relationships, so you should show them why you can deliver on all of those counts.

Set milestones, provide regular updates, use a project management system. Whatever it takes to ensure clean management of expectations.

Respect what you do when it comes to negotiation

You know the feeling, you gave a prospective client a price a couple of days ago which they've responded positively to overall and you can sense they're about to push the button.

Just one problem, they want a 25% reduction to the quote you've put forward, with some vague justification normally in and around 'it's just you and one other provider but I want to work with you'.
90 out of 100 freelancers in this instance will *take the hit.*

This is a fundamental problem. You're setting a precedent of weakness and the client is demonstrating bad apple characteristics. At this point you should respect what you do enough to push back against the proposed cost.

You'll find that most relationships will begin with negotiation, the longer-lasting partnerships are the ones built on mutual understanding and a win-win situation, hence its not healthy to start on the back foot feeling undervalued.

This is easier said than done of course but if you are to stick rigidly to your position as partner and to put a strong counter argument forward you'll often find your argument is strong enough to win the deal. A great way to counter this specific objection is to throw in two compromise options:

- Something *value-add but low impact* for free if you stick at the same price.
- Offer to match the price just slightly reduce the scope of the project

This shows a spirit of collaboration without undermining the respect you have for your own work or the value you've already demonstrated.

In closing

To close off this idea, you should view every client dealing as if it's the start of a five year relationship, spot the early signals of bad apples and look to cement longer term partnerships with clients who understand your sensitivities and show willing to build something more tangible long term.

In doing so, you can build enough repeat custom from your current pool of clients to get some way towards your stability goals.

Understand the purpose of side projects

As a freelancer, passenger on the "Income Roller Coaster" you should definitely be doing what you can to **multiply lines of income** to diversify your risk. I believe in this area so much I built a whole course around it at Handiwork.io.

You'll be hard pressed to find any *big business* brand that sells only product, or offers one single service. Technology brands sell hundreds of types of electronic products, farmers grow several species of crop and coffee shops don't just offer one single beverage.

Google for example has a motto "do one thing really well" – yet it owns YouTube, Gmail, Android, Google Docs and more and sits as the pre-eminent technology company in the world. Did I mention they have a search engine too?

Nathan Barry was looking for a way to augment freelance design earnings and saw the successes of other freelancers releasing books.

"I didn't know that someone like me, with no blog audience or following could make money off of a product until I saw two designers, Sacha Grief and Jarrod Drysdale release design ebooks and make $6,500 and $8,000 in the first 48 hours respectively"

You have a unique opportunity - as a service provider with a bank of expertise and experience to call upon – to wrap up that handiwork and expertise into a sellable package that can deliver you a diversified secondary / tertiary income stream.

The most difficult part of building a project like this of course is separating out the time it takes to create it. So in line with our commitment from earlier in the book, try setting aside 2 or 3 hours per week to work on content, products or projects that will elevate your opportunities to stabilize income in the long run.

Defining a product and understanding formats

In its simplest form a 'product' is a *pre-built embodiment of your skills and experience.* This can take the shape of a book, ebook, video course, podcast or simply just a bundled version of your own skillset. I've broken out the main formats, with pros and cons in the next section, but here is a summary explanation of what we mean when we say 'products'

A Book
Distributed physically or via Kindle / iBooks, this will be a 150-250 page book covering circa 30-50,000 words. You have in your hands, an example of this

Notable Examples:
Paul Jarvis – 'The Good Creative' (UK version)
Dan Norris – 'The 7 Day Startup' (UK version)

ebook
Generally promoted and sold via your own web channels and shorter in length, ebooks can be packaged with additional options or be sold in isolation.

Notable examples:
Nathan Barry – 'Authority ebook'
Brennan Dunn – 'Sell yourself online'

Video training
Building out your learning map into a series of videos and supplementary learning information.

Notable Examples:
Shawn Hesketh – WP101.com
Liam Veitch - Freelancelift

Productized service
You have several facets to your service and the job you do, often you can isolate out an element of that service and promote that as a product in its own right. This reduces the time cost of your service and productizes the deliverables.

Notable Examples:
Rob Williams – Workshop *(Isolating the 'finding leads' element)*
D Bnonn Tennant – Copy Bundle *(Isolating the 'Homepage copy' element)*

As a freelancer you're advising, teaching and solving problems on a daily basis for your clients, could you productize that advice or problem solving? Then you're putting out fires in your own life, could you take that load off your peers?

Workshop is a great example, it is a real drain to have to continually find new leads, and therefore Robert's service is almost a no-brainer to his designer peers. They will actively pay to have you remove that element of their role.

If you have lots of questions relating to a certain element of the service you're offering could you build a quick response library? Could you build that library out into a series of training videos for other freelancers answering those questions?

Could you build that library out into a book or an ebook? Could you ultimately sell that to people?

You should be thinking about how you can *solve problems by proxy* and in such a way that it can be created without a huge amount of work on your part, in the next section we'll look at the pros and cons for each product format in order that you can get clarity on which might be right for you.

Product format pros & cons

Book – Pros

Comprehensive

A book is comprehensive, much more so than an ebook. This provides a good amount of inherent credibility for your message. Everybody has read a book, everybody probably owns a book and so there is a high value placed on the production of one, since we're all aware of the sheer amount of work it would take.

Virility potential

A great book has the potential to go viral, just ask *now household* names like Tim Ferris and Ramit Sethi. Before their book releases they were mere *online entrepreneurs* or *bloggers*. Now they're 'New York Times Bestsellers' and TV personalities.

There is also the financial upside of going viral. Sure, your book may only net you $7 per sale but what if you sell a million copies? These are lofty expectations of course and extreme examples, but this potential exists still.

Instant self-publication (KDP)

An underestimated advantage is ability to instantly publish without a publisher, something unheard of even a few years ago. It's a huge step, only made possible by the advent of Kindle and iPad reading.

Kindle Direct Publishing is Amazon's direct upload platform, but you could equally use a middleman like Smashwords to upload your book to be syndicated through all stores at once.

Credible

Right now books are regarded as more credible than ebooks, a mindset hangover from a time when traditional publishing was selective and extremely difficult.

If you have your name on a shelf (even an electronic one) and have published reputed book in your industry you'll no longer be referred to as '*John Smith*', instead you'll be '*Author of X, John Smith*'

If you are looking to multiply your exposure then this precursor to your name and associated credibility can give you the extra leg-up you'll need.

Book - Cons

Limited on revenue

The most you can get away with asking for on Kindle and iBooks is probably $20 – with around $10-11 being the median price. Moreover, you're actively encouraged by Amazon to run a period where your book is *free entirely* on KDP Select. This means you have to make some serious sales to make a life-changing amount.

The market *demands* that books are below $20 – it's just not possible to list a $299 book on Amazon.

Sure, you could sell a million copies and it's possible, just not hugely likely as a first time author.

Very time consuming to create

How fast can you type? This book is 50,000+ words long. My typing speed is around 70-80 words per minute, so even if I were to type full speed without breaks for thought or research it would still have taken me 10 hours to complete.

As it goes I probably invested more like 100 hours into this project, if you could only commit 2 hours each week to writing it'd take you a year to finish.

8 million visits per day is no guarantee of success

Sure, Amazon and iBooks have a hefty amount of passing trade daily but don't be fooled into thinking this is a license to print money. There are far too many books uploaded daily for your book to succeed with passing traffic alone.

You'll need to put in the work to promote the book yourself, so you'll need to factor this time in as an additional cost to producing a book.

Ebook - Pros

Creating an ebook is the most common vehicle for teaching an outcome online. They are the easiest to create and distribute (via PDF) hence their popularity

Intended for PDF
ebooks are intended for PDF and that's very much the expected format. This means at its most basic level you can create your product using Microsoft Word alone and so it's a great place to get your feet wet with building a product.

Can be short and punchy
An ebook can be punchier and therefore easier to create than a book. If you have a set of objectives for an ebook laid out you can pad it out with illustrations and imagery that tell the story. Ultimately this ensures that a lack of content doesn't harm the overall impact of your content.

You should aim for 5-10,000 words for an ebook. If you're active on your blog you've probably written blog posts of 1,000+ without breaking a sweat so an ebook length should be very much within reach.

Quicker to produce
If you only have a couple of hours per week to be able to put something together, then go for an ebook. It'll enable you place your tentative first step on the ladder and get something *shipped*. Something you can point out as your own work that you can ask people to buy.

Once you get your first customer, you'll have the bug; building an appetite to try more complex product ideas.

Easier to bundle & create tiers

Nathan Barry advocates creating *tiers* of products to maximize revenue. So if you start out with an ebook you might add interviews, templates, frameworks, and screencasts to beef up the packages that follow.

As you're delivering them via your own site or through a service like Gumroad – unlike with a book - it's easier to deliver packages of bundled extras.

No real limit on price

At its simplest level, a price is a fair evaluation of the value contained with your product. If your product unlocks an extra $10,000 per month in revenue for the buyer what is a fair price? There is really no limit on ebook prices; that is to say if you're doing a good enough job demonstrating the value of what's inside your product then price becomes easier to justify.

Ebook - Cons

Not as credible as books

As the barrier to entry is significantly lower there is less credibility earned by creating a shorter guide. We all understand how much easier an is to create and so an ebook does not carry the same badge of authority.

Lots of noise and online competition

The biggest strength of an ebook (ease of production) is also its biggest weakness in terms of the opportunities it opens up for your competitors. This makes it difficult to stand out if you're not doing a great job of differentiating yourself.

Harder to justify value

Given there is no *real limit on price* this is something of a paradox. If your framing and value-proposition is not on-point you'll have a hard time convincing a prospective customer to even part with $12. There is no market force driving pricing (as there is with books) so your price lives and dies by the value you can attach to it.

Video Training - Pros

Video training on your own site or via Udemy or Skillshare is one of my favorite formats for spreading your message. If you've ever had a video or audio transcribed you'll find it amazing the amount of words covered in such a short space of time. You also have the power of *inflection* and *personality, which* is very difficult to replicate as quickly with the written word.

New technology brings lower barriers to entry
Had this book have been produced 10 or even 5 years ago, 'access to equipment' would definitely have been a con. You'd have had to lay down a hefty deposit for equipment hire and have needed to enlist the help of trained professionals to enable you to create a product worthy of distributing.

Nowadays though you probably have a High Definition video camera in your pocket, then you can grab a great lavalier microphone from Amazon for less than $20 and a lighting rack for under $50.

These are the baseline raw materials needed to produce great looking video.

Virtually unlimited pricing ceiling
There are video products you can purchase today that break the $10,000 barrier. This probably isn't going to be the price you aim for, but it shows that there really is no upper ceiling. Some products for example have access to hours and hours of video content so value can easily be demonstrated.

In reality, for a freelancer your upper limit is around $300-400 for the video content alone but the point to take away is that there will be fewer objections with higher cost video based products as there is an obvious time investment to produce it.

Easier to bill monthly for

Video translates best to a recurring model. Treehouse for example has built a huge business from *pay-monthly video training*. Fizzle.co is a newer runner in the race but now has over 1,500 users at $35 per month. It would be more difficult to drip-feed written content in this way.

Easier to demonstrate and justify value
Something we alluded to in the previous point is that video has inherent value as it offers a transparent look at the learning materials, with personality attached.

You can't really relate to the author chained to their desk to produce the book, but you can literally *see* the creator of a video product earning their living. This builds empathy, which can be leveraged to justify the value inside of a product.

Easier to portray a marketing message
With video its much easier to *'show don't tell'*. This approach when applied to the marketing of your product can be really powerful. Great video trailers on sites like Kickstarter have been the make-or-break factor of whether a project meets its funding goals.

Ultimately in Kickstarter a creator is *marketing* their project to an audience. The video makes it easier and more impactful to convince that audience to part with their hard earned.

More trust in a message
You'll be assured more trust and credibility just from the human empathy factor. If you're reading a book or an ebook, you do get a feel for the author but not nearly as much the quick impressions you're able to make when you can *see* them.

These are body language subtleties and personality cues that just don't reveal themselves in the written word.

Video Training - Cons

One of the most time-consuming to produce

It takes a lot of time to produce even a 5-10 minute video. When you consider putting together the script, equipment setup, editing, re-recording and finishing, that 5-minute video could take an hour or more to produce.

When your video course is 40+ videos (as Handiwork is) that workload soon mounts up.

Requires expertise that may be beyond your own

When it comes to *getting stuff done* I am more of a doer than a delegator, yet even I need to enlist extra expertise from time to time.

With the best will in the world you may still need to recruit external help, whether that is someone to hit record, to edit your videos, to create the titles or any other skill you will need come to terms with the fact you probably won't be able to do it on your own. This might be a blocker if your budget is tight.

No guarantee of success

Even with guarantees in place of a greater level of empathy, higher potential price point and fewer objections, video is not a guarantee of success. It still has the same pre-requisites as other products in the sense that success directly comes down to your positioning, promotion and persuading.

Can easily fail with poor execution

We've established that video, more than any other medium provides instant trust and empathy and a first impression factor that's difficult to replicate. So how do you think that is diminished when the video quality is shaky, sound is poor, the teacher is not very effective and the marketing is woeful?

With video there is a much finer margin for error, so consider that video production needs to be done professionally, for it to be done successfully.

Productized Service

Breaking down your service into smaller chunks, so as to productize the deliverable is perhaps the least common format. It can be best described as *breaking apart* the steps in your normal process into bite-size pieces you can sell in isolation. This is one of the more difficult to comprehend, so I've included a few more examples of service providers making this work.

Web Designer
Offer a design critique report and/or new conceptual design idea
Like Tom Ross – PushStandards - $197

Developer
Stress test and safeguard a WordPress site
Like Dan Norris – WPCurve - $69/m

Marketer
Marketing & promotional strategy session
D Bnonn Tennant - Information Highwayman – $299

Writer
Copy analysis and recommendations
Joanna Wiebe – Copyhackers - $1,000

In all of the above examples, the freelancers would carry out this work before or during a project anyway, however in these cases this isolated element has been commoditized.

On an overall project you may earn $2,000, but could you command $199 for an isolated selection, 5% of your service? If you can, and assuming you can sell 20 of these you in effect double your earnings for the same overall time cost.

Pros

You're doing it already
You're already delivering 100% of the service, so why not break it out and focus only on the bits you enjoy from the projects you work on?

Less preparation of an actual 'product'
Provided you have positioned what you do and have already established the value, your 'product' really is just your time. You will have a need to create a template for the deliverable and a process for delivery, but there is significantly less preparation and much smoother production.

Easier to execute on
Even though you're still technically swapping time for money; you can adopt a much more formulaic approach to your work. This repeatable process also ensures key elements can be outsourced as the need demands, to enable the ability to scale up volume.

Productized Service - Cons

Potentially limited audience
You may find that there are very few people actually *looking* for this problem to be solved. That is to say you have the first introduce an audience to the problem created by *not* investing in your product. This is a much more difficult task than justifying a solution to a more common pain.

Has a natural price ceiling
Unless you're celebrity in your space, you'll find it difficult to get buy-in for a productized service that costs *more* than your full service. That is to say if your product only solves 10% of the problem yet is 100% of a customer's budget your audience appetite is limited.

This 'ceiling' however would still represent a huge increase on your like-for-like rate for delivering this minified service as part of a wider project.

Still requires your involvement
If your goal is to make your secondary income passive or self-sufficient then productizing your service is probably not for you. Likewise if you are operating near capacity on a consistent basis then you'll struggle to prioritize the products over the full service.

In this instance I recommend you consider a productized service to be a hybrid of primary and secondary income, falling somewhere in the middle.

Getting on the path to creating a product

I created a platform specifically for freelancers looking to build products; Handiwork so it would be impossible for me to lay out everything in this book (or it would be twice the length) but here are the 10 main questions you need to ask if you're considering building out a product:

1.   What's the big idea?

Most great products are considered "great" because they are timely, impactful and solve a problem in a counter-intuitive way.

This fresh perspective or "big idea" once mapped out throughout your marketing and wider customer facing message could be the difference between building something that is "just like the others" and "changes the game".

2.   Who (specifically) will buy it?

This might feel a bit *business 101* but it's super-important. Just like your freelance service, your product customer should not be "the Internet" instead it something more specialized. *"Two person Swahili speaking businesses in the publishing sector"* anyone?

The more specific you are about your customer the less competition you'll have and the more likely it will be that you'll build a "category of one", to help reduce competing noise and get the attention of your prospective customer.

3.   What problem does it solve?

You should be solving a problem that is both **specific** and **regular.** We humans have a knack "putting up" with minor issues and light pain; we're very adaptive and inherently tolerant. So you have to speak to a real pain-point, not just something that happens 'every now and again'.

4.   Where do they hang out online?

Whilst you're getting into the mindset of your specific customer you should do some work to understand exactly where they hang out online.

This will give you the perfect cognitive ammunition to *think the way they think* and consider how you might intercept the circles they frequent, to capture their attention and drive them back to your message.

5.   How will you pull these to your offer?

In line with number four, if they are frequent Facebook users you could leverage display ads on the platform.   Likewise if you're familiar with the popular blogs in the space you can place display ads or guest content in those locations.

6.   What is their "tipping point"?

Your ideal customer right now is at point A. This is their status quo, with a regular, specific pain. Point B is their enlightenment, the point at which the problem is solved and they are happy.

Very few of your customers will be at point A when you're selling them your solution. The Internet has brought an army of "doers". We all naturally take to Google each time we need a problem solved.

So at what point along their information-gathering journey will they get stuck?

What is the most common sticking topic? They have restrictions that will prevent them getting past a point of 'self-treatment', if you can swoop in at that "tipping point" and show them the path to their enlightenment you will garner instant authority, credibility and be in the driving seat to make the sale.

7.   Why should they trust you?

We are all naturally very guarded. When we find ourselves in an unfamiliar place online, especially when someone is requesting money, we initiate the primal area of our brain that makes quick decisions based on the information available.

You need to convince someone quickly and concretely that you have authority and they can trust you. How will you do that?

8. How will you frame your offering?

Your solution might be as "boring and straightforward" as the humble car is a "practical mode of transport" but as with the framing analogy from phase two, when did you last see Mr. Ferrari advertising his new model as "good for getting from A to B"?

You need to tell your audience *how* this will improve their lives, bring in emotion, how will you overcome their problems? What is their "David moment" of beating their Goliath?

9. What is the resulting USP?

You should pull all of this data into a well-crafted set of simple sentences. This is your key differentiator and should explain fully and clearly precisely what the advantage of your solution is and what exactly it is you solve, and will almost certainly be unique from the 'difference statement that describes your service.

10. How will you turn this into revenue?

This is the fun bit, how much will you charge and what is the model? Are their similar products you can anchor your price to (higher or lower?)

Getting out there and doing it

When I spoke at length with other freelancers like you in the beta phase of Handiwork, 69% of them had tried to build a sideline product (a book, ebook or other method for productizing their freelance expertise) yet only 40% of that bunch indicated *they were happy* with how it went.

Not having a clearly defined audience is one of the most common reasons freelancers fail or get disheartened with side-project products. What else could be wrong?

Does the product suck?
Maybe – but if you struggled to make sales in the first place there were not many customers to tell you it sucked.

Is the freelancer somehow unqualified to teach the solution?
I don't think this is the case either as almost everyone has value to give from his or her experiences. Sites like Udemy and Skillshare showcase animators, illustrators, designers, writers and marketers all making modest sideline income from training products.

So what *is* the problem?
In almost all cases there is a serious problem with the way the product is being presented to an audience. Sure, your product should be awesome and indeed you should have the teaching abilities to help your buyer achieve their goal but if nobody values it more than the money in their pocket there is almost always a problem with **clarity of message.**

You can only have a simple, clear proposition if first you know specifically **who** will buy the product and what they *really* care about.

Sure, your product might be teaching ***advanced logo design for Illustrator*** but is that their real problem? Do they really care about that?

Did they really wake up this morning looking for yet another Adobe training course or is their real concern *the projects they keep on missing out on because their logo portfolio isn't quite where it needs to be?*

I call this the 'surface problem' – this is the real pain point your audience will be looking to remedy (whether consciously or not).

Your job as a 'creator' is to build a clear message around this 'surface problem(s)' that walks your prospect through why this surface problem is actually a symptom of a deeper problem, an 'underlying problem' they might not know they have.

Would you like to win more logo design gigs? You need to know more about this style of design and I can show you how.

VS

Would you like to know more about Illustrator? My product is…

The second version will inspire the ignore reflex and a reaction of *"No – leave me alone"*

Once you're clear on this and you build a clear message that **frames these surface problems as symptoms of an underlying problem** you'll have a much better proposition, which you can take to market.

All-told, products can provide a great way to augment freelance income by grouping together things you're already doing, into a product which can exist without being tied to you or your hourly rate.

Enabling stability by leveraging choice

The wildly successful daily cartoon strip series *'Dilbert'* has amused and inspired readers for over 25 years. Scott Adams - the artist responsible - is better known as 'Master of the Strip' in illustration circles and in February 1994 he put pen to paper to immortalize the concept of *'bullshit bingo'*.

The rules of bullshit bingo are simple; listen out for common jargon, clichés or idioms then call out 'bullshit' when your pre-created card is full.

When I find myself on run-of-the-mill freelancer platforms I often wish I had a bullshit bingo card of my own. There are some great resources for freelancers, however most are *patently average* and really don't give us any genuinely new insight.

One such buzzword is the often-empty advice to "just raise your rate" or "why not charge double".

Without appropriate context this well-meaning guidance serves no purpose, other than making us feel a little silly for not having billed more in the first place.

Put simply, *it's just not that easy* or we'd have done it already. Of course it's easy to add a zero to your proposal and hope for the best, but something feels wrong, uncomfortable without justification and as we're ultimately held hostage by revenue we're petrified of the client walking away.

The important words here to keep in mind are **justification** and **choice.** In phase two we talked about proposal and pricing strategies.

Those ideas still stand, we now have a solid foundation and you should be comfortable billing on the value you're bringing to the table but now we're looking at enabling stability not just raw *project price* uplifts.

How recurring revenue enhances client lifetime value

As a partner, you should already be doing what you can to maximize the lifetime value of each of your clients by looking towards the long term and by investing in the relationship.

This is especially helpful for repeat orders for the same product, but what opportunities do you have for maintenance options, retainers, 'refresh' work, consultancy or other value-add activity a client can be given the choice to sign up to? How many of these options are you offering?

Maintenance & support option

At Tone we offer a three-month bug fix period as standard with each of our site builds. This gives the client some comfort that we're not just waving goodbye to them once the project is over. Tapping into this same sense of reassurance we also offer an annual support contract.

For 15% of the overall project cost we'll be on hand for an unlimited amount of fixes and any other general query that can be resolved in less than 20 minutes. The client pays monthly for this security and reassurance.

Even on a basic website cost of $10,000, this provides us with $1,500 per year, or $125 *each and every month.*

The clincher here is that we have an uptake rate of about 70% on this, we frame it as a complete no brainer, a security blanket with a direct line into a simple ticketing system and someone who can take care of *anything they need, at any time.*

Then guess what? A client will often use this time sparingly so there is no major drain on resource as a result.

This applies to any industry and is a completely alien concept to most freelancers. So add an option for *ongoing support* to your next proposal, make sure you frame it as a no brainer option, being sure to speak to the worldview of the client and filling in the gaps in their knowledge.

If they are generally not tech savvy talk to them about keeping a CMS updated or by preventing malicious attacks.   If they are new to your area, talk in and around training or 'help by email'.   If they are time-poor frame it as a service to help them do the things they can't, like reminding when its time to do certain activities.

The psychology of choice here will help you have at least a 50% uptake on this option.

'Setup as a service'

In almost every industry there are tools and software platforms, which would make your client's life easier. They either never get around to setting them up or don't know how.   Whether its social media management, financial upkeep, cloud storage or display marketing there are tools and software platforms your clients are not using.

If you're doing a good job of establishing yourself as a partner already why not extend that within your proposal, to set up 'life saving' software on behalf of your client.

You should make this cost negligible or even free if you can, and here's why.

Most of these platforms have partner schemes, that is to say *you bring them a customer, they pay you a share.* I'm amazed that freelancers often don't make this leap.

The idea is simple; once you have agreement with a client that they'd like to take that option within your proposal you can register for the affiliate scheme of the platform you're going to set up.

You'll be given a link that you can provide to the client with explicit instructions (most platforms will give you a discount code in any case so as to make it difficult for the client *not* to sign up via your link).

When they register, you'll get paid, either monthly or as a one-off fee. This is great for building up baseline revenue as some partner platforms are really generous. Here are some examples

Project management – Teamwork.com – 25% of monthly subscription
Customer service – Zendesk – 20% of monthly subscription
Accounting – Freshbooks - $100 per account activation
Social media management – Hootsuite – 15% of monthly subscription
Domain names – GoDaddy – 10% per sale + 40% per new customer
Hosting – WPEngine - $200 per sale

You'll find some great options for monetizing software installation with affiliate platforms like Shareasale.

Consider this, if you're able to implement this for just *one client per month*, setting them up on two pieces of $50 per month software you'll earn around $2,000 over the year in commission alone at the average 25% rate, then if you bill each client $149 for the setup service you tap into further $1,800 in that period. This gets us an average of $300 per month closer to our 'stability' revenue.

Retainer option

Maintenance and support is easy to justify, it gives your client security and access to you for an unlimited amount of short, simple fixes and responses.

An extension to this is to offer a *retained* option to your service. That is to say, a regular, agreed piece of the work (or time allocation) at a reduced rate based on a longer-term commitment.

So if you're a writer, this could be a monthly blog post to extend out your services, if you're a web designer this could be bi-weekly split-testing to boost conversions, as a marketer this could be weekly analytics review.

You are ensuring value within partnership at this point, putting in place a formal agreement with clear activities, which you can frame as building momentum and ensuring your client is not left behind by their competitors.

Web hosting

Web hosting is a great value-add for your proposals, often it can be simple to persuade a client to opt for hosting for their project and the value is easy to justify, even if you're not in the web field.

When it comes to using hosting to facilitate stability there are two options.

The first way, if you're comfortable with the technical aspects (perhaps as a design/development freelancer), is to host your client's sites on a server you own. You can purchase a cloud server for around $40 per month.

If you re-bill your clients around $25 per month for this privilege you have the ability to quickly build up a pool of recurring income. This is especially attractive to clients who prefer the 'hands off' approach as you can just incorporate this into your service as an additional line item. Over the course of a year you may end up with 15-20 clients on your hosting platform, which provides you recurring income of maybe $500 *every month*.

The second, potentially simpler option is to register on an affiliate basis with a platform like WPEngine. With some of the best technical support I've witnessed, and ***prepared to pay you $200 for every new client you bring*** this should be a no brainer.

Indeed, this notion came up on a Freelancelift Q&A call with prolific freelance writer Tom Ewer of **LeavingWorkBehind**. Tom will extend his service by offering a 'free blog setup' option. For no additional cost, he'll handle the domain configuration, setup WordPress with a theme that looks good for the client's market, migrate in the content he has created, install relevant plugins and ensure everything works well, **at no extra cost.**

He can afford to do this – and not be bankrupt - as he makes a clear stipulation, they have to use his *recommended* hosting supplier.

The setup takes around 30 minutes but his client sees this as superb value, then with a platform like WPEngine or Bluehost (Tom's choice but not mine, as the commission on Bluehost is slightly less than WPEngine) he can earn $175-200 in commission for the new customer.

For this value-add aspect of his service, he's *earning $350-400 per hour.*

Consider how you can extend your service to include hosting and register with WPEngine to have this provide you with the stability you need.

Discount based on referral

If your market is well-tuned enough, you can simply ask the client if they'd like to take a 'partner option', that is to say you'll take 5% off the cost if they introduce you to somebody like themselves, who maybe in the market for your service.

Admittedly this actually takes away from your project cost in the short term, but what it provides is a new lead for every client win you're getting and if you win at least one in every four of these referrals you are on course to generating the additional 25-50% monthly amount to get to a point of stability.

Download full versions of the tools, resources and worksheets which support this book, by heading to freelancelift.com/book

Phase V

Loosening the reins, working less, earning more

A lot has changed since 1796. I often wonder what the burgeoning empire-makers of the early Industrial Age would make of today's world.

In that year an 18-year-old playwright by the name of Charles-Guillaume Étienne made his big move from rural France into Paris. Like Jeff - from earlier in the book - Charles had *intent* on his side and would eventually taste success, yet he applied his intent very differently.

Despite his young age, Charles-Guillaume had held several official positions in his municipality, residing over the tumultuous French Revolution. Following the country's fateful restructure, peace broke out and he moved his dreams to the big city.

Charles had a reputation for working into the small hours - a micro-manager or perfectionist in today's vernacular - and after a solid decade on the Parisian performing arts scene he coined a phrase, which embodied an attitude all too familiar to freelancers, of working 'in' a business rather than 'on' it:

"On n'est jamais servi si bien que par soi-même."

You may not recognize the French version, but in English this phrase was interpreted - and quoted widely for over 200 years since - as:

"If you want something done right, do it yourself."

This mantra feels common as freelancers, we do everything in our business and our organization chart is *Me - Me - Me* from top to bottom. I often play this game with freelancers during coaching calls.

- Who does sales? *Me, of course*

- Who handles inbound enquiries? *Me, of course*
- Who does the craft? *Me, of course*
- Whose responsibility is it to write content and do marketing? *Me, of course*

I'm amazed at how often we wear this mantra with pride. There seems to be the sense that it's *coming with territory* and we should embrace it.

I fundamentally disagree and I've been able to prove that an opposite attitude, putting processes and efficiency first is **significantly more effective**, especially when deep down our desire is to build a business that can survive without us in it for 12 hours per day.

When the question of enlisting collaborators, remote team members or local assistance is posed, it's met with the same fervent rejection Charles-Guillaume would have agreed with over 200 years ago:

"It will only take me a few minutes and after all, if you want something done right, do it yourself, right?"

If our aspiration - as a solo business owners - is to work less and earn more we're going to need to change that mentality. I have a better way, which ensures that we structure everything we do so that it can be:

- Made more efficient
- Handled by software
- Managed by someone else

This is the final phase of freelancer business evolution and something that I've been able to perfect for myself, freeing me to spend more time away from my business. We all have within us the ability to drastically cut the time we spend working within our businesses, it just takes a little perspective and an ability to block out the things holding us back.

I can forgive Charles-Guillaume for his misappropriation of time; his environment is very different to ours. In an age when you can leverage computing, software, instant global communication and 200 years of innovation it's not something I can forgive *you* for.

So let's make that change.

Your time has value

The first step in loosening the reins, working less and streamlining your business is to actually to understand that *your time has value*, something I think everyone struggles with.

Yes it'll be quicker and less hassle to do *that 30-minute task* yourself every other day, and yes doing so won't 'cost' you anything but contrast that with investing two hours, once, diligently teaching someone how to do that task *on your behalf.*

After an initial bedding in period, this task is eliminated from your list and moved to someone else's. The time adds up, did you know that a task taking 30 minutes every other day is actually 78 hours over the course of a year?

In that hypothetical scenario, migrating that one task in isolation opens the door to *$3,900* in extra revenue each year (imagining you bill $50 per hour).

Every time you *'just do'* that task - or *'do a Charles'* as I'll henceforth call it - you're squandering an opportunity to **do something else**; earn more with client work, go on vacation or just work less. Doing this task, albeit with no monetary cost brings this 'opportunity cost', a missed chance to do something else.

This is the mindset shift I'd like you to consider taking with me.

In this phase we'll look at understanding *where* your time is spent, we'll group this between revenue generating activity and non-revenue generating activity. There are some things we *just have to do* as businesses, but nobody says that *only us* can do them.

Simplistically, the only way to 'work less while earning more' is to do swap time spent doing 'non revenue' activities with work you get paid for completing.

Consume less, focus more

How many email lists are you subscribed to right now? What do you think would happen if you unsubscribed from all of them? You should look to do a quick tally, by checking through your last few weeks of email to list out all of the individuals and businesses you receive email from regularly.

It's likely you'll be on over 20 mailing lists. Assuming you receive at least two emails from each list every week you have *40 distractions* over the course of your working week.

That's one every single hour.

It would be impossible to action every piece of advice you subscribe to, so why let it become another precursor to procrastination, pinging your inbox every hour?

I advocate putting aside four or five hours per week for your own business development, therefore whatever you are consuming should not distract you away from allocating this time. If it does, it's a distraction to your objectives and is causing you to lose focus. Put another way, it isn't contributing so what's the point?

This *focus* is baked into everything I do at Freelancelift, so while I'm not advocating dropping *all other subscriptions* I'd like you to at least think about the sheer volume of ideas that are competing for your attention.

I challenge you to filter all of the emails you're receiving in order that distractions are minimized.

If you have Gmail you can quickly allocate subscription based emails into a list by simply adding a + to your email. Example: **johndoe+ideas@gmail.com**

You can then set up a filter to place everything marked with +ideas - or +subscriptions as another example - into a list, which will remain unopened until you can tackle these as a batch.

This is a close second to unsubscribing from everything

Understanding where your time is currently spent

I frequently comment on the similarities between time management and weight management and though the analogy does have holes in places, the similarities between the core concepts are uncanny.

Keeping a time diary

A couple of years ago I took on a personal trainer, the first thing he did was point me to an iPhone app, sat me down and explained:

"We need to understand exactly what you're eating on a daily basis, so we can evaluate, then eliminate the foods that make you retain fat. From there we can have you double up on the beneficial areas of your diet which you actually enjoy consuming"

Like weight management, time management begins with this **evaluation phase** and like weight management it's where most of us stop.

A large majority of freelancers I teach this to have never looked it this way, instead preferring to head straight into aggressive time management techniques picked up from some YouTube video. This is the equivalent to ducking past the nutritionist and heading straight for the heaviest dumbbell on the rack.

You might be able to lift it once, but you won't stick to it and you will *see no change* even though you felt the intense strain of effort.

Actually doing it

Without reservation I'd recommend Harvest for managing your time diary. There are other platforms such as Rescuetime which tracks application usage in the background, automatically but you are limited in breaking out tasks into sub-tasks with this platform, both are free however.

You can use a good old pen and pad though if you find it difficult to commit to managing the app tracking.

Retrospectively tracking time
If you're champing at the bit to start immediately (or if you forgot to record over a couple of days) you can track time retrospectively by:

- Looking back through old 'to do' lists
- Checking your diary for your movements on the day(s) in question
- Checking your received/sent email as that probably will align with what you were doing at the time
- Checking your recent calls on your phone to check for call durations and caller IDs

The purpose of this (admittedly menial) activity is to get clarity, for potentially the first time on where your time *really* goes. Activities you used to think took you 'half a day' actually end up only taking a couple of hours, while 'quick tasks' we all complete may end up swallowing hours without you knowing.

If you're tracking your time correctly you'll start the head slap moments almost from day one, *"did I really just spend 37 minutes looking at my Facebook feed?"*

For the best possible insight, you should be categorizing tasks into macro and micro activities so you can be really clear on time spent. Try getting as granular as you can so your data is as accurate as it can be.

Example of Macro vs. Micro activity

Macro

- Publishing a post for your blog
- Taking a client call or email and arranging a Skype appointment
- Meeting a prospective client for a pitch

Micro

For publishing a post for your blog
- Thinking of blog topic ideas
- Taking a look at what is popular on other sites
- Creating the content
- Adding in imagery and adding to WordPress
- Publishing the post and sharing on social media

For taking a client call or email and arranging a Skype appointment
- Answering the call or receiving the email
- Taking notes for the call
- Adding the notes to your CRM
- Adding a meeting to iCalendar

For meeting a prospective client for a pitch
- Research on the client's specific needs
- Creation of slide deck
- Attending meeting

You'll find that every macro task probably has 5-10 micro (sub)tasks and it'll quickly become clear that for a large swathe of these sub-tasks your involvement is not absolutely necessary, but we'll come to that later.

Are you doing 'empty work'?

You'll already be familiar with the term 'empty calories' as it relates to nutrition, denoting food, which contributes calories but provides no nutritional value, some fats and sugars for example.

'Empty work' is the time management equivalent; the mysterious black hole stealing minutes and hours from under your nose.

Every time you hit "Send/Receive" on your e-mail client and nothing shows, each time you aimlessly refresh your Twitter or Facebook feed, every time you watch a video or read a blog post which provides more questions than answers.

There is a place for social media and industry reading of course and email is essential, it just shouldn't *define* your day. Taking social media as an example, if it does not contribute to the forward momentum of your business and if you struggle to recall what you actually contributed then you're guilty of doing empty work.

The rule of thumb here is whether at the end of a day you can recall what you did on social media and specifically why that mattered. If you can say, "I contributed to the LinkedIn group on XYZ, resulting in two likes and 10 visits to my site" then you can class it as useful activity, which contributes, to your goal.

If its an "ummm, ahh" then you're probably stuck doing empty work in 'serial refresh' mode.

Time perception

The good news about holding yourself responsible for your time like this is it will naturally unearth a hidden *productivity ninja*. The first step, when it comes to time management and productivity is eliminating distractions and working for fixed periods of concentration.

When you understand empty work and put in the necessary logistics to accurately track your time your time perception and 'self-protection' instincts will exponentially improve.

All of us with smartphones can relate to subconsciously checking email at inappropriate times, over dinner or midway through a conversation.

By working with the clock rather than against it you're acutely aware of what you *should* be doing at that moment in time. This tunnel vision and commitment is what you should be working towards, zoning in and actually **getting shit done.**

In doing so you become clear about how your business operates and how much of your time it really demands.

Perspective on what's really important

My wish for this part of the book is to give you a little perspective on the
processes at play in your business.   If you've recorded where your time is
being spent over the course of two or three weeks you may have 25-30 rows of
activities. For a practical next step you should be able to allocate each task
into one of the four groups below.

**Group 1. Generates revenue and it's essential I carry out this
activity**
For example; fulfilling your service or meeting with clients

Group 2. Generates revenue, but it isn't essential I carry it out
For example; strategic marketing activity or sending invoices

Group 3. Does not generate revenue but it is essential I do it
*For example; attending industry Google Hangouts or conversing on social
media*

Group 4. Does not generate revenue and it isn't essential I do it
For example; maintaining financial records or publishing a blog post

The yes/no diagram will give you a flow to cross-reference tasks against, when
it comes to defining whether it absolutely requires you is to ask yourself the
question "Could someone do this 80% as well as I could with basic training?"

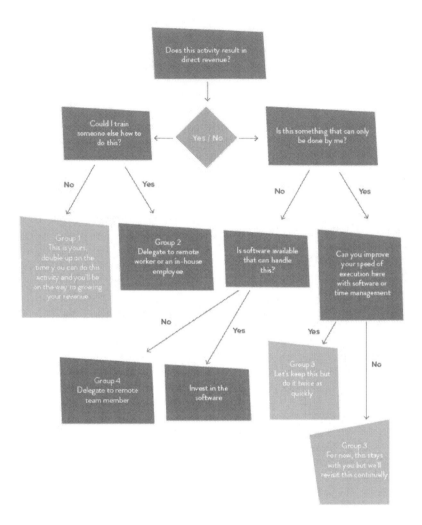

Leveraging technology

We live in an innovative time, what was considered 'enterprise level' software five years ago is now commonplace among freelancers and small businesses.

That is to say you have a unique opportunity to leverage technology to maximize your efficiency as a business and often it takes *tracking time* to unearth where these savings could be made.

Leveraging people

The landscape for leveraging the support of *people* is becoming easier to comprehend every day. How many tasks have you identified within tracking which really do not require your undivided attention to complete and don't contribute to your revenue objectives?

Optimizing yourself

Can you improve the speed at which you can execute on tasks? The yes/no chart should be able to identify where you can optimize your own efficiency, either by cordoning off distractions or by building slicker processes.

Leverage the support of a remote team

Adii Pienaar founded one of the most successful businesses to grace the WordPress theme space, WooThemes. In doing so, he built a team of employees dotted around the world.

Adii grew his team slowly, building delegation and teamwork into the heart of the business. One key takeaway from a recent Freelancelift Q&A call was the quick sense check I advocated earlier in the chapter, *"Can this person do this 80% as well as I could?"*

Accepting that as an individual you can't do everything, you should look to build systems and processes you can hire into, this supports any new team member with repeatable, easy to follow systems to follow.

Understand that for some activities in your business, your hourly rate – which may be $50 or more – is simply not appropriate or most efficient. There are great remote workers, across the World in varying disciplines able to lend a hand for $5 to $10 per hour.

It's vital to remove all preconceptions before making this commitment to outsourcing appropriate activities so as to work less while earning more.

Overcoming remote-team preconceptions

Certain preconceptions may be holding you back from achieving the time freedom you're really looking for, here are some I'd like to reverse.

"Living costs are lower in this area so I can get this work done for $1 p/h"
The first and most common assumption about outsourcing is that you work pretty much hands-off, via faceless communication methods, pay peanuts and get the most menial tasks imaginable completed.

This is just plain wrong, in fact when you consider the career options of intelligent, well-educated, multi-lingual young people in developing nations such as India, Philippines, Indonesia their options are wide-open. They have made a conscious decision to go it alone and launch a freelancer business of their own.

That is to say you're actually working *entrepreneur to entrepreneur* not *paymaster to subordinate* and just as with any service related business 'lowest cost' almost never results in 'highest quality.'

"I need to post a new job every time I need something doing "
This isn't true. You can either distribute tasks on a project basis to a wide field of remote team members or hire individuals for an agreed period of time each. In either case, it's vitally important to build strong relationships with preferred providers.

"Its their job to understand what I want and then just do it"
As I hinted at above, you really need to look to a remote team as an *extension of you*. If you provided poor instructions to an employee sat right next to you and denied them an opportunity to clarify, or worse still berated them for even attempting to reconfirm do you think that'd be a good induction to your business?

When working with remote team members, this courtesy is just as important

"This task only takes me 10-15 minutes by the time I've explained it I'll have done it"
This might be true, but if a task is regular, then these chunks of time when combined really add up. By developing processes and instructions for team members you can have these tasks completed elsewhere so you can re-invest that time on activities, which potentially deliver more value.

"Outsourcing is just for admin duties right?"
In almost all areas, freelancers and small businesses underestimate the value of specialists. Yes, the majority of your timesaving will be achieved by outsourcing your 'non-revenue non-essential' (group 4) activities but you might be surprised how much further a good team member will be able to go.

For example, who's to say you're the best at writing that blog post? Or researching a client's requested solution? Could someone manage your PPC budget better than you could?

Don't look at outsourcing just as a tool for getting rid of admin, instead consider how *experts in specific fields* can help you function better as a business.

We're looking to build a team that is agile and able to scale with your business in order that you can loosen the reins, and work less while at least retaining revenue. This is at the core of this phase and enables you to part with a "do it yourself" 18th Century attitude.

Departmentalize your tiny business

Every business task normally falls into one of three main business disciplines. This is something your tiny, one-person business has in common with corporate giants. These can then be broken out into 'departments', as the lists below demonstrate.

Right now, responsibility for each block in this organization chart lies squarely with you. This is unstable and potentially unsustainable, when you are unavailable every single department is effectively closed.

Sales & Marketing
- Attraction & Conversion
- Customer Retention
- Product Management
- Reporting
- Market Research

Operations & Infrastructure
- Finance
- Human Resources
- IT & Systems
- Customer Service
- Administration

Production & Fulfillment
- Service Development
- Service Delivery
- Service Improvement

You'll always be heavily involved with actual service delivery and for some of the more engaging aspects of marketing, but you're probably in a position to extricate yourself from a whole host of tasks within *Infrastructure* along with the more administrative areas of *Sales & Marketing*.

Only by looking at your business as a series of processes, backed by clear evaluation on how this relates to your time can you start to consider the business surviving without you in it.

It's quite liberating when you start to see this come together as you're finally starting to work "on" your business than "in" it.

I regularly revisit this exercise, tracking where my time is spent and departmentalizing it before simply asking the question, *could I deploy software to help here or train someone to do this activity on my behalf?*

If you were able to save just 10% of your time on a weekly basis by leveraging a team, software or productivity improvements, this is 192 hours clawed back over a 12-month period assuming you work 40 hours per week.

That's an ***entire working month*** saved over a year.   How could you re-invest that time?

The power of processes

Whether the objective is to deploy software, leverage a remote team or increase your speed of execution, it is vital to understand each process along with define the point at which every one of them is carried out.

Processes underpin everything that you do and sometimes they're subconscious.

A process, or system, is a *sequence of steps working towards a defined result or outcome.* Retuning a process can be the key to improving how you work, making your chances of success - when our objective is to work less, or more efficiently - infinitely greater.

For every task there is a process and regardless of whether this is explicitly known or identified it still exists. Understanding this fact and being able to assess each link in that 'system' can really help you propel to maximum productivity, fix long-term problems and enable you to work systematically rather than on a haphazard basis.

When processes fail

Whenever you have a problem, or fail to achieve a desired result you can probably track it down to a broken process. A step has failed, or the wrong step is being implemented and this is preventing you from reaching the ideal outcome.

There could be several problems with the process, or just one, but there will always be at least one step preventing you from reaching the goal, so lets take a look at how you address this and ensure you can avoid falling foul of broken processes in the future.

1. Identify the problem

We'll go through a specific example here, a struggle with a particular remote team member you're outsourcing work to.

So your starting point is that your hire *isn't up to scratch*, they are under-delivering and time keeping is an issue.

2. Remove the who, make it a "what"

When trying to fix a specific problem like this, the first step is to identify the process at work and how you got you to that point in the first place.

You should remove all elements of 'who' and find the root issue, reframing your mindset to instead look for the 'what' and determine *what* in the process has failed. Could more have been done at each step?

Could the budgeting step have been better, to allocate a higher cost to get a better qualified team member? Could you have done better job of laying out their responsibilities? What about the selection phase? Maybe the interview step? Maybe the onboarding? What about the ongoing communication?

As you can see, there are several steps along the way, which can be broken out and reviewed sequentially. Understand what you did - or didn't do - at each step and consider how it leads to the next one. At this point you'll probably uncover some glaringly obvious fixes. *'Wow, I didn't even do a job specification'*

It should hopefully become clear which steps are problematic and preventing you reaching your goal. The next step is to change those steps or improve them to get the process back on track.

3. Understand your ideal outcome

You can't fix a process unless you really understand the ideal outcome, what should have happened?

Expressing this is the only way to identify which step has gone wrong and come up with a new - or much improved - one, which will help you to reach your goal and outcome more quickly, better and more profitably.

Using our example, the ideal here would be that a remote worker *joins the business and is empowered to work autonomously and deliver great work, on time.*

3. Build a new process

Armed with the insight as to where you feel your process failings are, you can build a new process, which addresses every broken link and every possibility of failure.

I recommend a swim lane process map structure. They are super-effective at separating out individual responsibilities.

4. Put it into effect

This is the fun bit; you can now hit the reset button on that particular problem in your business, starting again with your refined process.

You'll quickly find that although there may be some additional work in the early stages of developing your new processes the new steps you've added will help you in the long term by freeing up time and energy to push forward and fix new problems.

Learning from both your strengths and your weaknesses

Don't just look at problematic areas to find processes. Identify areas you succeed in, or are very productive in, and try and understand the process here. See if those process can be migrated to other areas, so that you can achieve the same success elsewhere. You should learn from your successes too, not just your failures.

Fully understanding the processes you follow (consciously or otherwise) will help you improve and fix them, providing boosted productivity and a clearer perspective on business constraints.

Outsourcing diligently

By agreeing to do every role in your business you leave yourself exposed to stress, under pressure from distractions and provide yourself with invalid justifications.

By tracking your time, departmentalizing the resulting tasks and grouping them by revenue and non-revenue generating activity you have the blueprint for building a more profitable business structure.

Your available platforms

Elance

Elance is one of the most popular platforms and is my recommended for laborer assistance. You do get a mixed bag on Elance but within the deluge you'll receive are some gems. The trick is to choose carefully, the right professionals can assist you on your business journey.

Elance (which has now merged with oDesk) has an active community in web technology, programming and administrative assistance but is equally strong in all areas. As with all platforms filtering is your friend, Elance in particular has great tools for you to be able to grade, segment and otherwise interrogate the proposals you're receiving.

PeoplePerHour

I've found PeoplePerHour to be excellent for writing and content in general. It's great if you're looking to outsource proofreading, creative writing, ghost writing and so on.

Mechanical Turk

Excellent for high-volume labor-intensive tasks. If you're looking for assistance with research or data entry, this channel is very effective.

What makes for a good response?

The first thing you'll receive from your would-be team member is the proposal. If this is a template, thoughtless proposal you can easily discount or ignore their response.

Sometimes the shorter the proposal, the better, as they're addressing your key concerns head on without copy and pasting en masse.

Look out for
- It's custom-written and reads well (not necessarily the longest)
- You are addressed personally
- The provider is well-reputed

Internal or remote?

One of the best things I did was take on physical staff members early. It was 2011, I was doing well and could have just *'played the freelancer'* busily managing all business activities and working my ass off 10 hours a day.

My brother, Adam was out of work at the time having attended university so I offered him a few days work every week to help me manage the load.

He would take care of the administrative duties that web designers often need to get their hands dirty with; chasing the client for content and getting this migrated into their WordPress CMS.

Adam was able to take the slack too with social media updates and keeping on top of the aspects that would help keep attention high. I highlighted that I would struggle to keep those particular plates spinning while I had other client work taking my time.

I'll not disclose his salary but suffice it to say it was manageable for the fledgling business at that time and it freed me up to do more of the work that delivered revenue, resulting in a positive investment from the outset.

As workload grew Adam switched to full time and I was joined by another friend, Anthony who too was in need of a change in direction career-wise.

Both of whom now have over 3 years web agency experience under their belts, are an asset to the business and could go and get a job in any agency in the country.

It's too easy to discount 'real' team members when you're a one-person business but my advice is to start small, casually employ people you know, help out a friend or younger family member who would find the arrangement mutually beneficial.

Your objective is to work less, and earn more by working only on what's important – it's quite possible to shed 20-40% of your workload by delegating this activity to other team members, leveraging software or maximizing your efficiency.

Maximizing your own efficiency

Get good at email inbox management

There are numerous, often conflicting methodologies around how best to manage email. My personal preference is to just close the email client for periods when concentration is in order and only check once per hour or so.

A close second is *Inbox Zero*. If you're familiar with the Inbox Zero methodology, it leverages as the Four Ds:

- **Delete** it
- **Do** it
- **Delegate** it
- **Defer** it

That's a great way to manage emails, or "processing" emails which is a better explanation of roughly what's happening. Inbox zero is sometimes a little hard to keep on top of however but I hope it serves to give you some idea of the gains you can make by achieving a faster speed of execution.

If you're on Gmail there is an excellent new app simply called Mailbox, which brings the power of *Inbox Zero* into an iPhone app. Their unique concept of "snoozing" certain emails is a masterstroke!

Understand the value of UIHD

A killer tip from Chris Johnson of Simplifilm is to utilize the UIHD technique, it's a simple way to ensure more efficient communication with clients as well as a more fluid workflow with outsourced support.

With it you're basically taking away the need for your recipient to reply with "yes" or "that's fine" for low-impact decisions you're already 60-70% sure are correct.

When freelancing these short delays (sometimes a client can really hold up the simplest of decisions unintentionally if they are unable to get the time to reply) can be the difference between hitting a deadline and not. When deadlines are tied to final payments time is money so the more of it you can save the better chance you have of making freelancing that bit more stable.

You'll have to set the expectations initially so your clients know when to expect it and how they can react but once you pass the agreed point, the decision is considered made.

Adopt a 'lean' mindset

In his book 'The Lean Startup' Eric Ries introduced a whole new vernacular for the tech startup space.

The idea behind 'running lean' actually lies in cutting waste and focusing on the smallest possible effort for the maximal possible gain. A standout idea was that of the MVP (minimum viable product) which looks to dispel the notion that a solution or business needs to be 100% perfect before going to market. In *The Lean Startup*, Ries instead advises to go with the least amount of features you can get away with, then build, improve, innovate your idea from there.

I talked to author Brant Cooper on a Freelancelift Q&A call, around relating this back to freelance businesses, to do everything it takes to push your business forward without over-committing or presuming.

That blog post you're deliberating over, **publish it**... those clients you're procrastinating over contacting, **email them**. If your approach doesn't work, you at least have a benchmark set of results to work from and improve.

Getting it done

Starting ignition on your journey

I've been able to build something incredible from my tiny freelance business and in this book I've poured out everything I wish I'd have known then.

This is where our journeys overlap; the final chapter of this book should be the first chapter of your evolution towards building your freelance business into something that can provide a stable, enjoyable and exciting living.

Reading and absorbing the contents of this book however will only get you so far, you need to put the keys in the ignition and take the next steps yourself.

I've built Freelancelift as a constant beacon to your success though so you're welcome to continue your journey by leveraging this platform but just remember why you started and why you chose to buy this book in the first place.

Belief

You need to believe that this is possible, we've spoken about the opportunities that are out there; you'll surpass 90% of all freelancers even if you only implement half of the ideas in this book. You have the creative capacity to take this on, so do so with earnest, gusto and passion.

Commitment

Do what it takes to commit to evolving your business, one step at a time by allocating hustle time every week to develop your business and break away from maintenance mode.

Concentration

The framework I've built ensures you have the quickest route to building a product, however it does require that you apply concentration every time you engage with your product build project.

You should work to block out distractions and invest in your *"Me Project"*. This is something I've talked about at-length on Freelancelift and throughout my Q&A sessions with some of the brightest entrepreneurs in the space – in particular Corbett Barr, who advocates this strategy, to develop your Me Project, to invest in yourself and to build something that moves you and your business forward

Breakthrough

I've seen products provide the breakthrough for many businesses and it can prove to be yours. You may be familiar with the software platform Basecamp, well 37Signals' initial success came in the shape of a PDF book 'Getting real'. This generated the income that supported the business as it grew to the software titan it is today and CEO Jason Fried publicly considers this a breakthrough for the company.

Ultimately, one mile is 63,000 inches. You're not going to get where you need to go incrementally, one inch at a time.

You need to make the big compound moves to ensure a breakthrough, to get that lifestyle you're really looking for and to build the revenue stream that you otherwise don't have.

Just don't fail

In closing, I just wanted to give you the red flags I now live by. **I've failed plenty of times.** Indeed, I thought I'd never make it back to freelancing after almost losing the shirt on my back about five years ago.

As we all do, I tried to 'stem' the losses and offset freelance earnings by jumping on bandwagon after bandwagon, dreaming up fanciful ways to supplement my income from online channels. All this gave me though was a *cover for procrastination*. This 'opportunity seeking' took me away from committing to the work which really mattered and which would potentially have turned my fortunes around.

This book will give you all of the pieces you may be missing, if you can avoid the lure of the 'easy out' you'll have it within you to make it work, and build something incredible from your tiny freelance business.

I published for all to see the 10 things I learned failing spectacularly as a freelancer, and this is a fitting way to exit this book.

Even as a freelancer, you're not exempt from that word, "business" so you should care about continually correcting your course, cataloguing prior micro mistakes, rolling up your sleeves and ultimately minimizing failure potential.

I'm 100% sure I'll have lots more over the next 5-10 years but here's where I'm at so far, so here we go.

1. Too much faith in the magic bullet

This is a biggie, something I encounter a lot when I speak to Freelancelift members. There was a time when I was on 27 mailing lists, probably 5 or 6 direct mailers and I'd enrol on some online wonder-programme or other almost on a monthly basis.

What I quickly realised was that even though each probably had some merit it would be physically impossible to action everything. I was chasing the magic bullet, the quick win, the 1%, the 'never never'... resulting in getting quickly 'nowhere nowhere'.

How I beat it

I unsubscribed from all lists, installed a kick-ass anti spam and began my list amnesty. Anything I felt lost without, I resubscribed to and I put more emphasis on actually finding my own information, only following content creators who spoke my language.

I succeeded at only seeking expertise when I needed it rather than being force-fed generic information which only distracted me from achieving my unique vision. This enabled me to work out my own solutions with good old trial and error backed with only credible guidance.

Your own beaten path is much more reliable than an off the shelf "insert-superlative-here" whizz-bang system
How you can beat it

Commit to getting better, not consuming every hot new idea which requires a rework of the way you do things. Take yourself off the drip feed of mindless email lists, use your intuition and follow credible voices who won't try and ram a programme down your throat at every opportunity. Then you'll finally be able to save yourself from drowning in content you'll never be able to action.

Some picks to rebuild after 'list-amnesty' – Corbett Barr & Chase Reeves at Fizzle, Justin Jackson, Bidsketch, Tom Ewer

2. Lack of self control

Aged around 18-21 I took the "lifestyle business" to the extreme.

I woke in a daze one Tuesday morning at 11am to the conclusion that what I'd built was all lifestyle no business, I mean who wants to think accounts and forecasting after a 5 day weekend?

But I was young at that point (9-10 years ago), finding myself and some of that stuff did help the creative juices flow which took me down the perennial path I'm still meandering today.

If you're aiming for a business which supports your lifestyle you should double down on strategy & efficiency to ensure you are able to physically "cap" your working week. When you add in a dash of self control you won't squander the working time you've set forth, preventing that sinking feeling you get from not putting in the work.

How I beat it

Oddly enough things started to change for me when I actually "went to work". Previously I always had a home office.

I hired a desk in a shared co-working environment which enabled me to divide my business/personal life in a more physical way. The nice sidenote is that in the 3 years that have followed the floorspace I now occupy (with my awesome team at Tone) in the same building has increased by a factor of 20 with 16 desks at last count.

How you can beat it

Try to channel friends with high self control & will power. We all know the guy who refuses midweek drinks, who always considers how decisions affect tomorrow and the next day or the gal who hits the gym 4 days a week no matter what. Study what makes them tick and see if you can mould it to your own personality. Then try to look beyond the 'home-working' thing, even as a freelancer. Co-working spaces are really cheap and they offer secondary benefits such as referral opportunities as you build up a network in the space.

3. Ambiguous goals

This is something I pound the drum about a lot. The fact of the matter is some would-be entrepreneurs go into freelance business just to make money, without clearly understanding and defining what makes for success.

"if you don't have a map, compass or destination how do you intend to get from A to B?"

When I started out alone aged 19 I knew I needed to make enough to pay the bills. In the end I did, but as I didn't have a clear vision for success and I stuttered into a plateau which, combined with failpoint 1 commenced a downward spiral in my fortunes.

Had I been able to track performance against realistic goals, consider my business journey evolution rather than growth I could have taken more decisive action to stop the rot.

How I beat it

For every new project or venture I undertake I'm doubly clear on what I want to get out of it. These goals are time sensitive and very specific. This helps me to be objective about progress and allows me to pat myself on the back every now and again!

How you can beat it

Your journey as a freelancer doesn't need to be such a mammoth project, you just need to work backwards from your monetary goal and understand what that looks like in terms of customers, order value, prospects, visits, online visibility.

You also then need to be specific about what your lifestyle looks like so you can continually be auditing yourself, ensuring you're not sacrificing living the life you want by chasing it.

4. Overcomplication, start small

One of the best moves I made when freelancing second time around was doing it part-time until I could justify enough earnings to go full-time. With an embryonic vision in hand, I set about putting together a new part-time design business. I was motivated by one vow: to try again, and do it properly this time.

On Freelancelift I put lots of ideas out there, the key takeaway from this to start implementing these ideas in small, manageable chunks. You don't have enough hours in the day to put everything into play immediately, so start small, test new ideas and continually evolve.

In the early days I tried everything, each time going "all in" putting my neck on the block daily. I over complicated ideas and gave up on most as a result. This is a waste of time in the long-run so I'm here to tell you to scale down the complication, start small and test it.

How I beat it

I made myself known in the freelancer marketplace, part-time at that, which enabled me to work with pretty much bare bones until I proved the concept and found my particular space.

Once the concept is proved jump in with both feet, until then don't over invest in it.

How you can beat it

Definitely think set aside only a small amount of time for business development alongside your current activity, definitely try leveraging a remote team, definitely start small and really pin down your vision before fully committing and you'll beat overcomplication.

5. *Poor grasp of time value / leverage*

This was one of the major catalysts in my recent years' business growth. I won't go too much into it here as I've got tons of extra resources on the topic of leveraging 'Big Business Stuff' and processes but essentially you need to understand this:

As a business owner you wear lots of hats. Doing everything yourself for 'free' is false economy; damaging to the well being of you and your business.

Understand that everything in your business can be mapped out into a process and you can leverage a remote team to get things done to deliver on that process.

How you can beat it

The penny dropped when I devised a yes/no flow (which you can follow yourself here) building a business flow to help me deliver items which didn't immediately require my attention, but in summary you need Stop thinking like a freelancer, start thinking like a business.

6. Sacrificing vision in face of difficulty

So here's the thing. I'm a sucker for great branding, purposeful self-promotion and really clear, unbridled vision.   But what happens when times get tough? What about when you need to cut costs, do things faster?

I found myself pawning out my brand and quality of delivery in return for quicker revenue or lower costs, running your business like this is the quickest way to end up with 'bad apples'. Poor quality clients you don't enjoy working with.

How I beat it

It's a real tough one and I'm not sure I fully have but at least I'm aware of it when it rears its head. The one benefit I have though is ability in every area of my business interests. That is to say if everybody who worked at the businesses disappeared I could probably manage, even stripping it right back to me and my laptop.

I'm very aware this flies in the face of the distributed workforce and lifestyle business but I guess the learning point for me on this one was to always have a plan B and to know enough about what you're doing to be able to survive.

How you could beat it

In some of my content I talk about "devise the what, outsource the how" that is to say you make the big calls, devise the processes and have an arms length understanding of every point of your business but your team deliver on that vision.

If you make your team members accountable for documenting their work too you'll be in a much better place to safeguard against disasters.

7. Lack of software availability

I used to spend 15+ hours per week on activities such as:

- managing accounts
- calculating payroll
- emailing "nearly clients"
- sharing files by snail mailing CDs / USB (yes, really)

This is something that couldn't really have been avoided at the time as most didn't exist beyond the realms of $10k / month enterprise software but current technology allows huge timesavings by really getting good at software.

How I beat it:

Almost all of the above is automated and second nature now, last year I was invited to share our software stack on Under30CEO – what's interesting is that this software is almost all free.

You should leverage as much as you can to ensure you can take advantage of the closing gap between Enterprise level software and 'off the shelf' cloud platforms.

8. All optimism no realism

Part of the entrepreneur's makeup is ambition and optimism. On the surface the two are the same but in the past I've been guilty of allowing my ambitious streak to out-run realism, when it comes to decision-making.

That is to say I'm using my ultimate goals, my vision and ambition as a guide instead of cross-referencing with straight-up objective realism, potentially quite dangerous.

How I beat it

I now put together a 'what if' analysis for each major decision. For minor (mainly financial ones) I do a quick cashflow forecast to find out worst case scenarios. These aren't huge exercises, I've just developed a few simple questions to get to the core worst case scenario but the point here is to understand the wide spectrum of consequences for every major decision to protect you from any potential failure.

How you can beat it

You're probably doing this already but at the least, take no decision lightly – you should be able to make each decision with a couple of questions:

- Is this purchase/hire/contract/etc a contribution to my roadmap or a distraction?
- What is the worst case scenario of making that choice
- By using the steps above you'll be much more informed and be less reliant on your ambition or instinct.

9. Not being proud of it

As I've said above I've tried lots of business models. Some okay, some really spammy I'm not proud to say. From flipping domains to electronics dropshipping, from running affiliate sites to margin stock trading. You name an Internet lifestyle 'trend' I've probably tried it.

The traits the above have in common is that they were each:

- pretty darn ugly
- a failure ultimately

They all existed as a plot to make quick money, nothing more. I wasn't proud of them. I soon realised that the key to making business work is to be proud of everything you put your name to, and to use value as your shining beacon. This was one of the reasons I advocate ditching freelancer exchanges like Elance as quickly as possible, you'll not make work you're proud of with clients from those platforms.

Yes its longer term but if you're proud of what you have achieved and can be sure you're providing value to a specific sector as a freelancer you're on the right track.

How I beat it

Well, I was a creative at heart and knew what looked good so I pretty much self-taught Photoshop and started to take control of the branding of any new business ventures.

I also found that sharing what I was working on via my own immediate social circle (think close friends & family) forced me to check and double check what I was putting my name to.

How you can beat it

If you aren't a creative, find a good creative minded partner or freelancer to team up with. If you can provide the detailed vision, direction and product/service you can work together to package that up into something you can be proud of.

10. Not finding my own voice

This is a pretty recent one and in some way goes back to the point on chasing the magic bullet as it relates to being 'known in your space'. I wrote a short book "Why nobody knows your name" to outline how to grow your online reputation, in it I recall that in the early days I was mimicking other bloggers and web entrepreneurs rather than finding my own voice and personality.

I pretty much hid all reference to my age, my background, my face and everything that would allow the visitor on the other side of the screen to connect. The result was lots of copycatting, no fixed idea of my market, no engagement and pretty much no impact.

Your personality should come through in everything you put your name to and you should be able to provide strong points of view that reflect your own personal experience and outlook. Combine that voice with great content in a specialist area and you're on to a winner.

How I beat it

I guess this came with time and experience. As I was able to (over time) develop my own experiences rather than channeling someone else's I became more confident in what I was saying and a little more relaxed in my approach.

How you can beat it

You can begin to look at which styles of content / presenting feel natural to you. Is it long, deep, data-filled posts? Is it short opinion pieces? Are you more curator and do you provide more value that way? Are you better talking via a screencast? Or on video in front of a whiteboard?

Try stuff, see which firstly feels right, then once you're in a comfortable place see what resonates best with your audience.
At that intersection you'll find your voice.

Finally

I am not perfect and I have a lot more failures to endure on this path I'm sure, I've just mustered the endeavour and commitment to keep going, learning as I overcome each obstacle. I've not yet reached the end and as the old Churchill quote goes:

"Success is not final, failure is not fatal: it is the courage to continue that counts."

Winston Churchill

Acknowledgements

I'm fiercely independent, but even I know that no man is an island so first to my wife, Michelle.

We just had an amazing wedding in September 2014 and I'm looking forward to the next 60 Septembers.

To all of the team at Tone especially Adam, Anthony, Brandon, Jordan and Michael. Also Jean for good measure.

To David, fellow director at Tone. David doesn't feature too heavily in this book but definitely had a hand in making that $1M a reality as the business began to scale.

To Alec and Morissa for helping me stay on track and for making the book at least readable.

Tom Morkes of Insurgent Publishing for showing the light and shepherding the whole thing into production and to the perfect guests who are littered throughout this book namely:

Corbett Barr, Brennan Dunn, Amy Hoy, Nathan Barry, Shawn Hesketh, Justin Jackson, Robert Williams, D Bnonn Tennant, Adii Pienaar, Neil Patel, Paul Jarvis, Brant Cooper, Tom Ewer.

Thank you to the 200+ book ambassadors who helped spread the message upon launch and the 600+ others who registered their interest in an early notification for it's launch.

Finally, here's to 5,000+ freelancers bossing it inside Freelancelift.

Let's make something f'ing amazing.

Tool up

I wanted to make this as interactive an experience as possible, so I've complied all of the resources from the book into a page where you can download and implement.

Download full versions of the tools, resources and worksheets which support this book, by heading to freelancelift.com/book

Support the cause

Let me know how you found the book, use the hashtag #1mfreelancer and loop in @freelancelift, we'll see each and every one!

Stop thinking like a freelancer
The Evolution of a $1m web designer

15863912R00134

Made in the USA
Middletown, DE
24 November 2014